A Journey Into The Rich, Lavish World of Cheesecakes

To Jon,

Enjoy & happy baking.

Bruce A. Williamson

A Journey Into The Rich, Lavish World of Cheesecakes

Bruce A. Williamson

Icons of Indulgence, The Holiday Cheesecake

TATE PUBLISHING
AND ENTERPRISES, LLC

Published by Tate Publishing & Enterprises, LLC
127 E. Trade Center Terrace | Mustang, Oklahoma 73064 USA
1.888.361.9473 | www.tatepublishing.com

Tate Publishing is committed to excellence in the publishing industry. The company reflects the philosophy established by the founders, based on Psalm 68:11,
"The Lord gave the word and great was the company of those who published it."

Book design copyright © 2013 by Tate Publishing, LLC. All rights reserved.
Cover design by Allen Jomoc
Interior design by Jomel Pepito

Published in the United States of America

ISBN: 978-1-62510-426-7
1. Cooking / Holiday
2. Cooking / Courses & Dishes / Cakes
13.01.23

This book is dedicated to my mother, Rita, who taught me to bake at a young age. The patience and love shown in her teachings is reflected in this book. I'd also like to dedicate it to family and friends who had to endure eating all the cheesecakes.

Acknowledgments

I would like to express my deepest love and gratitude to all my family, friends, and acquaintances, especially:

Percy Boucher-Williamson, my wife, and our children Michelle, Deborah, and Christopher, who had to endure eating more cheesecake, in the last year or so, than most people eat in their lifetime. I want to especially thank my patient wife, Percy, who allowed me the many hours to write this book when I should have been doing other things. Thank you all for your faithful support, I love you dearly and I'm grateful for all you add to my life.

Vickie Hadge, my niece and typist, who so graciously took the time out from her own business to type this manuscript. Many thanks; you're the best!

Joe Jacobsen and Tito Badia, my wine consultants and pairing experts, who unselfishly donated their time and expertise to perfectly pair the ideal wine with each unique cheesecake. I'm forever in your debt!

Emma Bailey, my editor, who so willingly gave of her time to give the manuscript a meticulous going-over and for her constructive comments. I can't thank you enough, Emma!

John McManaman, my indexer, who magnificently accomplished the task of putting together the index for my book with professionalism and in a very timely manner. Many thanks, John!

Laura Stone, (of Laura Stone Photography) my photographer, who brought my cheesecakes to life and made their images alluring visions of decadence. Great job, Laura!

Ramie McDaniel, acquisitions editor, who felt a first time author's cookbook was acceptable for publication. Rachael Sweeden, director of operations, Cheryl Moore, graphic designer, Meghan

Gregg, book project manager, and all the talented staff at Tate Publishing, who put the finishing touches on my book and turned a dream into reality. God bless you all!

To all the taste testers (impossible to name you all), who were so anxious and willing to participate in this venture. I thank you for your honest, straightforward comments and opinions.

To the many authors on the internet whose articles, recipes, and facts provided the knowledge and understanding to be able to write this book.

Last but not least, the mystery person, who planted the seed for this project by simply saying, "Why don't you write a cookbook?" From there, it's all history. Whoever you are, God bless!

Contents

Introduction

*I*t's the holiday season again! So time to indulge, dig into your favorite foods, and celebrate nature's bounty with friends and family. This year, take an old-fashioned custom and make it new again. Why not give a twist to the traditional dessert fare and make it into one indulgent dessert—wonderfully rich, velvety-smooth, and irresistible eating experience that your guests will surely remember.

A cheesecake is one of those decadent desserts that's sure to bring your holiday guests to their knees; craving more because every bite is so creamy, delicious, and definitely worth every calorie.

These irresistible icons of indulgence make any holiday dinner special. But many home bakers perceive cheesecake as hard to make and are intimidated by a dessert this delicious and good-looking. A cheesecake is nothing more than a crust made from easy-to-find graham cracker cookie crumbs, and a filling made with cream cheese, sugar, eggs, and sour cream for added richness. Once cooked and chilled, the cheesecake can be topped with one of the many decadent toppings suggested in this book.

If you follow the techniques and tips described in the early part of this book, your cheesecake can be as easy to make as a traditional holiday cake or pie.

This cookbook with its collection of unique, original, and seasonal recipes has been written and planned to appeal especially to two groups of home bakers: those intimidated bakers, who are reluctant to bake a cheesecake even if it's their first attempt; and those experienced cheesecake bakers who are just looking for something new and different to add to their holiday dessert menu.

In this book, the recipes are geared for the first group, the reluctant bakers. The recipes are written in a format that is simple, easy to follow, and detailed—without being overly wordy.

Also, the recipes in the book are presented in a nontraditional format. A traditional formats lists all the ingredients in the order in which they will be used in the recipe, followed by the directions or procedure in which the product is to made and assembled.

The format I will be using breaks down the cheesecake into its elements: crust, filling, topping, and, in some cases, a secondary filling. The ingredients are listed in order of their use for each element, followed by its procedure. One reason for choosing this method is that many of the components in the recipes can be made one day or up to a week ahead of time. In several of the recipes, this method is strongly suggested so the individual flavors have a chance to marry, resulting in a more flavorful tasting experience.

When a recipe has a long list of ingredients, it can appear to be complicated and difficult to make. But when a cheesecake recipe is reduced to its individual components, listing only several ingredients for that element, its perception goes from intimidation to simplistic and will encourage your start in the world of cheesecakes.

Time is at a premium during the holidays! With all the other things we have to do in preparation for the coming events, this format can be used to spread out the baking time over several days if needed. The cheesecake can be completed on the day of your event or just before serving. Another option is to make the cheesecake a few days ahead of time and keep chilled until just before serving.

My intention, and purpose, in writing this book is to show those of you who are apprehensive, but immensely enjoy cheesecake, that it is no more difficult to make than any other holiday dessert.

Happy Holidays, and welcome to the rich, lavish world of cheesecake.

The Cheesecake

Cheesecake is a beloved dessert around the world. What you may not realize is that the original cheesecake looked and tasted nothing like what we enjoy today. While many assume that it has its origins in New York, it actually dates back much further. Before you sit back and grab another creamy slice of this tasty dessert, let's go back over four thousand years to Ancient Greece, take some time to learn about the cheesecake origins you never knew, and learn all about this dessert's rich history.

Ancient Greece-The Birth Place of the Cheesecake

The first "cheesecakes" were thought to be made in Ancient Greece, on the island of Samos. Archaeologists and physical anthropologists excavated and reported they found cheese molds there that dated back to 2000 BC—that means cheesecake is more than four thousand years old! Cheese and cheese products had most likely been around for thousands of years before this, but earlier than this goes into prehistory (that period in human history before the invention of writing) so we will never know. In Ancient Greece, cheesecake was not the creamy dessert treat we recognize today. In Greece, cheesecake was considered to be a good source of energy, and there is evidence that it was served to athletes during the first Olympic Games in 776 BC. On the Greek island of Delos, newlyweds were also known to use cheesecake as a wedding cake. The simple ingredients of flour, wheat, honey, and cheese were formed into a cake and baked—a far cry from the more complicated recipes available today!

The Greek writer Athenaeus is credited for recording the first Greek cheesecake recipe in AD 230. (By this time, the Greeks had been serving cheesecake for over two thousand years, but this is the oldest known surviving Greek recipe!) It was also pretty simple and basic: pound the cheese until it is smooth and pasty, mix the pounded cheese in a brass pan with honey and spring wheat flour, heat the cheesecake "in one mass," allow to cool, then serve.

The Romans Put Their Own Twist on the Cheesecake

When the Romans conquered Greece, the cheesecake recipe was just one of the spoils of war; they took the opportunity to put their own twist on the original Greek cheesecake recipe. They modified it including crushed cheese, instead of pounding it, and added eggs to the mixture. These ingredients were baked under a hot brick and it was served warm. Occasionally, the Romans would put the cheese filling in a pastry. The Romans called their cheesecake "libuma," and they served it on special occasions. Marcus Cato, a Roman politician in the first century BC, is credited as recording the oldest known Roman cheesecake recipe.

As the Romans expanded their empire, they brought cheesecake recipes to the Europeans. Soon, all of Eastern Europe and Great Britain was enjoying the cake. Great Britain and Eastern Europe began experimenting with ways to put their own unique spin on cheesecake. In each country of Europe, the recipe started taking on different cultural shapes, using ingredients native to each region. By AD 1000, cheesecakes were flourishing throughout Scandinavia, England, and in northwestern Europe. In 1545, the first cookbook was printed. It described the cheesecake as a flour-based sweet food. Henry VIII's chef did his part to shape the cheesecake recipe. Apparently, his chef cut up cheese into very small pieces and soaked those pieces in milk for three hours. Then he strained the mixture and added eggs, butter, and sugar.

It was not until the 18th century, however, that cheesecake would start to look like something we recognize in the United States today. Around this time Europeans began to use beaten eggs instead of yeast to make their breads and cakes rise. Removing the overpowering yeast flavor made cheesecake taste more like a dessert treat.

Cream Cheese Enters the Picture

When Europeans immigrated to America, some brought their cheesecake recipes along; little did they know they were opening this recipe up to one of its most distinctive changes. Cream cheese was an American addition to the cake. And it has since become a staple ingredient in the United States. In 1872, a New York dairy farmer was attempting to replicate the French cheese Neufchatel at his home. Instead of recreating the French cheese, he accidently discovered a process which resulted in the creation of the first cream cheese. Three years later, in 1875, the distinctive cream cheese was packaged in foil and distributed to local stores under the Philadelphia Cream Cheese brand. The Philadelphia Cream Cheese brand was purchased in 1903 by Phoenix Cheese Company, and then it was purchased in 1928 by the Kraft Cheese Company. Kraft continues to make this very same delicious Philadelphia Cream Cheese that we are all familiar with today.

New York Style Cheesecake

Of course, no story of cheesecake is complete without delving into the origins of the New York style cheesecake. The classic New York style cheesecake is served with just the cake—no fruit, chocolate, or caramel is served on the top or on the side. This famously smooth-tasting cake gets its signature flavor from extra egg yolks in the cream cheesecake mix.

By the 1900s, New Yorkers were in love with this dessert. Virtually every restaurant had its own version of cheesecake on their menu. New Yorkers have vied for bragging rights for having the original recipe ever since. Even though he is best known for his signature sandwiches, Arnold Reuben (1883–1970), owner of the legendary Turf Restaurant at 49th and Broadway in New York City, is generally credited for creating the New York-style cheesecake. Other bakeries relied on cottage cheese for their recipes. Reuben was born in Germany and he came to America when he was a young boy. The story goes that Reuben was invited to a dinner party where the hostess served a cheese pie in a private home, and he fell in love with the dessert. Using his hostess's recipe and a pie she made with ingredients he provided, he then began to experiment to develop his own recipe for the ultimate cheesecake. Reuben soon began to serve his new recipe in his Turf Restaurant, and the cheesecake quickly became very popular with his patrons.

Variations on Cheesecake in America

New York is not the only place in America that puts its own twist on cheesecakes. Pennsylvania Dutch cheesecake use farmer's cheese, which has bigger curds and more water than other kinds of cheese. In Chicago, sour cream is added to the recipe to keep it creamy. The "country style" version of cheesecake uses buttermilk to get more texture and increase the cake's shelf life. Meanwhile, Philadelphia cheesecake is known for being lighter and creamier than New York-style and it can be served with fruit or chocolate toppings. In St. Louis, they enjoy a gooey butter cake, which has an additional layer of cake topping on the cheesecake filling

Different Countries, Different Variations

Each country and region of the world has its own take on the best way to make the dessert, putting their own spins on the cheesecake. Italians use Ricotta cheese, while the Greeks use mizithra or feta. In Bulgaria, a cheesecake will be made with cream cheese and a heavy souring cream known as smetana. Germans prefer cottage cheese, while the Japanese use a combination of cornstarch and egg whites. French cheesecake uses Neufâchel cheese and gelatin to keep the cheese together. Meanwhile, in Poland, cheesecakes are made with fresh cheese known as quark. There are some specialty cheesecakes that include blue cheese, seafood, spice chilies, and even tofu! In spite of all the variations, the popular dessert's main ingredients—cheese, wheat, and a sweetener—remain the same.

No matter how you slice it, cheesecake is a dessert that has stood the test of time. From its earliest recorded beginnings on the island of Samos in Ancient Greece over four thousand years ago, to its current iconic status around the world, this creamy cake remains a favorite for sweet tooths of all ages.

The Cheesecake Pantry

*A*s the holidays rapidly approach, the pantry is one of the places you probably have stocked up with baking staples. Your cupboards and refrigerator more than likely have flour, sugar, spices, eggs, butter, cream cheese, vanilla extract, and baking chocolate. From there, it's not such a big leap into the wonderful, lavish world of holiday cheesecakes. Following is a guide to the ingredients you'll use most often as you bake your way through the unusual, decadent recipes of this book.

Being a chef myself, I am a firm believer in the commitment to the principle of "market cooking," used by such chefs as Alice Waters, owner of Chez Panisse in Berkeley, California and Jasper White, chef-owner of Jasper White's Summer Shack at the Mohegan Sun in Uncasville, Connecticut. They have a dedication to using the finest seasonal and organic (when possible) ingredients from local sources.

I have been working with the State of Connecticut Department of Agriculture Marketing and Technology Bureau to comprise a list of Connecticut grown and produced products that can be used in these cheesecake recipes. See the Appendix "Local Products Sources" at the back of the book for this list.

Butter

Butter is the product of churning cream until it separates, forming a milky liquid and solid butter fats. Butter is prized in the bakeshop for its flavor; however, it melts at a relatively low temperature (approximately 93°F) and burns easily. Unsalted butter is preferred for baking *because* it tends to be fresher, and additional salt might interfere with product formulas.

Chocolate

Bitter—or unsweetened chocolate—is straight chocolate liquor. It contains no sugar and has a strongly bitter taste. Because it is molded in blocks, it is also referred to as *block cocoa* or *cocoa block*. It is used to flavor items that have other sources of sweetness.

Sweet chocolate is bitter chocolate with the addition of sugar and cocoa butter in various proportions. If the percentage of sugar is low, sweetened chocolate may be called *semisweet* or, with even less sugar, *bittersweet*. Both of these products must contain at least 35 percent chocolate liquor, and their sugar content ranges from 35 percent to 50 percent. A product labeled *sweet chocolate* may contain as little as, 15 percent chocolate liquor.

White chocolate consists of cocoa butter, sugar, milk solids and vanilla. Technically, it is not chocolate because it contains no chocolate liquor. Use only high quality white chocolate for the best results in a recipe, making sure it contains cocoa butter, not vegetable oil.

Cookies

Purchased cookies are used to make delicious crumb crusts for the cheesecakes. Examples of cookies used in these recipes are graham crackers, gingersnaps, chocolate and vanilla wafers, and shortbread. The cookies are crushed or ground into fine crumbs, then combined with butter and usually some kind of sugar to form a moist, gritty texture that clumps together when compacted.

Cornstarch

Finely ground dried corn kernels that is white in color and silky smooth to the touch. Cornstarch is often used as a thickening agent. To avoid lumps, mix cornstarch with a cold liquid, then gradually whisk it into the hot liquid. For cornstarch to properly thicken, it must never boil.

Cream Cheese

Cream cheese is a soft, spreadable, unaged cheese that has a higher fat content, about 35 percent, made from cow's milk. It is usually the main ingredient in cheesecakes, which give them their rich flavor. Cream cheese is also used in buttercream frostings and toppings.

Examples of other types of cheeses used in cheesecakes are: cottage cheese, mascarpone (Italian-style cream cheese), ricotta (soft Italian cheese, similar to American cottage cheese), and Neufâchel cream cheese (French style cream cheese).

Dairy Products

* Cream—Is formed naturally when milk separates into two layers – a thick, creamy top layer with a thin milky liquid below. Various types of fresh cream differ primarily in fat content.

* Whipping cream—Has a fat content of 30 to 40 percent. Within this category, you may find *light whipping cream* (30 to 35 percent) and *heavy whipping cream* (36 to 40 percent)

* Sour cream—Has been cultured or fermented by adding lactic acid bacteria. This makes it thick and slightly tangy in flavor. It has about 18 percent fat.

* Yogurt is milk (whole or low fat) —Cultured by special bacteria. It has a custard-like consistency. Most yogurts have additional milk solids added, and some of it is flavored and sweetened.

* Greek yogurt—Is a type of strained yogurt, made by straining the yogurt through cheese cloth or a coffee filter to remove excess liquid.

Eggs

Eggs should be well understood by the baker because they are used in large quantities in the bake-shop and are more expensive than many of the other high-volume ingredients such as flour and sugar. For example, half or more of the ingredient costs of the average cake batter is for the eggs. Eggs perform the following functions in baking:

* Structure—Like gluten protein, egg protein coagulates to give structure to baked products. If used in large quantities, eggs make baked products tough or chewy unless balanced by fat and sugar, which are tenderizers.

* Emulsifying of fats and liquids—Egg yolks contain natural emulsifiers, which help produce smooth batters. Emulsifying contributes to volume and texture.

* Leavening—Beaten eggs incorporate air in tiny cells or bubbles. In a batter, this trapped air expands when heated and aids in leavening.

* Shortening action—The fat in egg yolks act as a shortening. This is an important function in products that are low in other fats.

* Moisture—Eggs are mostly water. This moisture must be calculated as part of the total liquid in a formula. If yolks are substituted for whole eggs, for example, or if dried eggs are used, adjust the liquid in the recipe to allow for the different moisture content of these products.

* Color—Yolks impart a yellow color to doughs and batters. Also eggs brown easily and contribute to crust color.

Extracts

Extracts are flavorful oil and other substances dissolved in alcohol. These include vanilla, lemon, bitter almond, cinnamon, and coffee.

Flour

Wheat flour is the most important ingredient in baking. It provides the bulk and structure to most baked products. The characteristics of flour depend on the variety of wheat from which it is milled, the location in which the wheat is grown, and its growing conditions. The most important characteristic of flour is protein content.

For our purposes, it is enough to know that some wheat is classified as hard and soft. Hard wheat contains greater quantities of the proteins called glutenin and gliadin, which together form gluten when the flour is moistened and mixed. Flour from soft wheat with low protein content are important in the production of cakes, cookies, and pies. *All-purpose flour* is a blend of hard and soft wheat; it is the most common flour used in home kitchens. It can be used in most baked goods, unless otherwise specified in the recipe.

Fruits, fresh

Botanically, a fruit is an organ that develops from the ovary of a flowering plant and contains one or more seeds. Culinarily, a fruit is the perfect snack; the basis of a dessert, colorful sauce or soup, or an accompaniment to meat, fish, shellfish, or poultry. No food group offers a greater variety of colors, flavors, and textures than fruit. The following are some of the fruits that will be used in the cheesecake recipes in this book.

* Apples—Perhaps the most common and appreciated of all fruits, grown on trees in temperate zones worldwide. They are popular for their convenience, flavor, variety, and availability. Apples can be eaten raw out of hand or they can be used in a wide variety of cooked and baked dishes.

  Apples are harvested when still slightly under ripe, then stored in a controlled atmosphere (temperature and oxygen are greatly reduced) for extended periods until ready for sale. Modern storage techniques make fresh apples available all year, although their peak season is during the autumn.

  When selecting apples, look for smooth, unbroken skins and firm fruits, without soft spots or bruises. Store apples are chilled for up to six weeks. Recommended apples for baking are: Honeycrisp, Jonagold, and Cortland.

* Clementine—A variety of mandarin orange. The exterior is a deep orange color with a smooth, glossy appearance. Clementines separate easily into seven to fourteen segments. They are very easy to peel, like a tangerine, but are almost always seedless. They are typically juicy and sweet, with less acid than oranges.

  Clementines are available from mid-November through January—causing them to often be called "Christmas Oranges."

* Cranberries—A native North American fruit, they are a tart, firm fruit with mottled red skin. They grow on low vines in cultivated bogs (swamps) throughout Massachusetts, Wisconsin, and New Jersey. Rarely eaten raw, they are made into sauces or are used in breads, pies, or pastries. Cranberries are readily available frozen, and fresh during their peak harvesting season from Labor Day through October.

* Currants—Tiny tart fruits currants grow on shrubs in grape-like clusters. The most common are a beautiful, almost translucent red, but black and golden (or white) varieties also exist. All varieties are used for jams, jellies, and sauces; and black currants are made into a liquor *crème de cassis*. Although rarely grown in the United States, currants are very popular and widely available in Europe, with a peak season during the late summer.

  Currants can be frozen by placing them in their container in a food saver bag and vacuum sealing the bag.

* Dates—The fruit of the date palm tree, dates have been cultivated since ancient times. Dates are about one to two inches long, with a paper-thin skin and a single grooved seed in the center. Most are golden to dark brown when ripe.

  Although dates appear to be dried, they are actually fresh fruits. They have a sticky, sweet, almost candied texture, and rich flavor.

  Pitted dates are available in several packaged forms: whole, chopped, or extruded. Whole unpitted dates are available in bulk. Although packaged or processed dates are available all year, peak season for fresh domestic dates is from late October through December. When you're selecting dates, look for those that are plump, glossy, and moist.

* Figs—The fruit of the ficus tree, figs are small, soft, pear-shaped fruits with an intensely sweet flavor and a rich, moist texture made crunchy by a multitude of tiny seeds. Fresh figs can be baked, poached, or used in jams, preserves or compotes.

  Dark-skinned figs are known as Mission figs. They have a thin skin, small seeds, and are available fresh, canned, or dried. The white-skinned figs grown commercially include the White Adriatic, used principally for drying and baking, and the all-purpose Kadota. The most important domestic variety however is the Calimyrna. These large figs have a rich yellow color and large nutty seeds. Fresh Calimyrna figs are the finest for eating out of hand; they are also available dried.

For the best flavor, figs should be fully ripened on the tree. Unfortunately, fully-ripened figs are very delicate and difficult to transport. Most figs are in season from June through October; fresh Calimyrna figs are available only during June.

* Kumquats—Very small, oval, orange-colored fruits with a soft sweet skin and slightly bitter flesh, kumquats can be eaten whole, either raw or preserved in syrup, and may be used in jams and preserves. Store kumquats refrigerated for up to two weeks.

* Lemons—The most commonly used citrus fruits, lemons are oval, bright yellow fruits available all year. Their strongly acidic flavor makes them unpleasant to eat raw, but perfect for flavoring desserts and confections. Lemon zest can also be candied or used in baking.

* Limes—Small fruits with thin skins ranging from yellow-green to dark green, limes are too tart to eat raw and are often substituted for lemons in prepared dishes. They are also juiced or used in cocktails, curries, or desserts. Lime zest can be grated and used to give color and flavor to a variety of dishes. Limes are available all year; their peak season is during the summer.

* Oranges—Round fruits with a juicy, orange flesh, and a thin, orange skin, oranges can be either sweet or bitter. Valencia oranges and navel oranges (a seedless variety) are the most popular sweet oranges. They can be juiced for beverages or sauces, flesh may be eaten raw, added to salads, cooked in desserts or used as a garnish. The zest may be grated or julienned for sauces or garnish. Sweet oranges are available all year; their peak season is from December to April.

* Peaches—Moderate-sized, round fruits with a juicy, sweet flesh, peaches have a thin skin covered with fuzz, with the flesh ranging from white to pale orange. Peaches are excellent

for eating out of hand or in desserts. They are also used in jams, chutneys, preserves, and savory relishes. Select fruits with a good aroma, an overall creamy, yellow or yellow-orange color, and an unwrinkled skin free of blemishes. Red patches are not an indication of ripeness; a green skin indicates that the fruit was picked too early and it will not ripen further. Peaches will soften and do become sweeter after harvesting. Their peak season is through the summer months, with July and August producing the best crop.

* Pears—An ancient tree fruit grown in temperate areas throughout the world, most of the pears marketed in the United States are grown in California, Washington, and Oregon.

    They are most often eaten out of hand, but can be baked or poached. Pears can be used in fruit salads, compotes, or preserves.

    When you are selecting pears, look for fruit with smooth, unbroken skin, and an intact stem. Pears will not ripen properly on the tree so they are picked while still firm and should be allowed to soften before use. Under ripe pears may be left at room temperature to ripen. A properly ripened pear should have a good fragrance and yield to gentle pressure at the stem end. Pears can be prepared or stored in the same way as apples.

* Quinces—Resembling large, lumpy, yellow pears, their flesh is hard, with many pips and seeds, and they have a wonderful fragrance. Too astringent to eat raw, quince develop a sweet flavor and pink color when cooked with sugar.

    Fresh quince, usually imported from South America or Southeast Europe, is available from October through January. Select firm fruits with a good yellow color. Small blemishes may be cut away before cooking. Quince will keep for up to a month in the refrigerator.

* Raspberries—Perhaps the raspberry is the most delicate of all fruits. Raspberries have a tart flavor and velvety texture. Red raspberries are the most common, with black, purple, and golden berries available in some markets. When ripe, the berry pulls easily away from its white core, leaving the characteristic hollow center. Because they can be easily crushed and are susceptible to mold, most of the raspberries grown are marketed frozen. They

grow on thorny vines in cool climates from Washington State to western New York and are imported from New Zealand and South America. The peak season is from late May through November.

Fruits, dried

Drying is the oldest known technique for preserving fruits, having been used for more than five thousand years. When ripe fruits are dried, they lose most of their moisture. This concentrates their flavors and sugars and dramatically extends shelf life. Although most fruits can be dried, plums (prunes), grapes (raisins, sultanas, and currants), apricots, and figs are the fruits most commonly dried.

Dried fruits actually retain from 16 to 25 percent residual moisture, leaving them moist and soft. Dried fruits may be softened by steeping them for a short time in a hot liquid such as water, wine, rum, brandy, or other liquor. Some dried fruits should be simmered in a small amount of water before use.

Store dried fruits in airtight containers to prevent further moisture loss; keep in a dry, cool area away from sunlight. Dried fruits may mold if exposed to both air and high humidity.

> Dried fruits can be stored in an airtight container at room temperature for several months or refrigerated in a tightly sealed bag for up to a year.

* Dried Coconut—Unsweetened, shredded, shaved, or chipped coconut flesh. Dried coconut lends a mild, sweet coconut flavor and texture to desserts and is often used as a garnish. After being toasted, dried coconut becomes golden with a slightly nutty flavor.

* Dried Figs—They come in two varieties: dried California figs, with thick beige skin; and dried black Mission figs, which have very dark skin. They can be used interchangeably in recipes. The figs should be sweet and relatively moist.

* Raisins—Dried grapes, usually made from Thompson seedless or Muscat grapes. Thompson seedless grapes can be used to make both dark and golden raisins. To produce golden raisins, the grapes are treated with sulphur dioxide, and then dried with artificial heat; golden raisins are fatter and moister. Raisins made from Muscat grapes are dark and very sweet.

Jams and Preserves

Fresh fruit can be preserved by cooking the fruits with sugar and sometimes pectin; preserves feature large pieces of fruit.

* Apricot Preserves—Apricot jam or preserves has a light amber color and is often used as a glaze for fruits and tarts. Apricot jam will be used as a glaze in some of the recipes in this book.

Nuts

A nut is the edible single-seed kernel of a fruit surrounded by a hard shell. A hazelnut is an example of a true nut. The term is used more generally, however, to refer to any seed or fruit with an edible kernel in a hard shell.

Nuts should be stored in a nonmetal, airtight container in a cool, dark place. Most nuts may be kept frozen for up to one year.

Nuts are used in foods and desserts to provide texture and flavor. They are often roasted before being used in order to heighten their flavor. Allowing roasted nuts to cool to room temperature before grinding prevents them from releasing too much oil.

* Almonds—The seeds of the plum-like fruit, the almond, were first cultivated by the ancient Greeks. Native to western India, it is now a major commercial crop in California. Almonds are available whole, sliced, slivered, or ground.

* Cashews—Native to the Amazon, cashews are now cultivated in India and East Africa. The cashew nut is actually the seed of a plant related to poison ivy. Because of toxins in the shell, cashews are always sold shelled. They are expensive and have a strong flavor.

* Coconuts—The seeds from one of the largest of all the fruits, coconuts grow on the tropical coconut palm tree. The nut is a dark brown oval, and covered with coarse fibers. The shell is thick and hard; inside is a layer of white, moist flesh. Coconut has a mild aroma, a sweet, nutty flavor, and a crunchy, chewy texture. Fresh coconuts are readily available but require some effort to use. Coconut flesh is available shredded or flaked, with or without added

sugar. A good fresh coconut should feel heavy; you should be able to hear the coconut water sloshing around inside.

Coconut milk is a coconut-flavored liquid made by pouring boiling water over shredded coconut; may be sweetened or unsweetened. Do not substitute cream of coconut for coconut milk.

Coconut cream is a coconut-flavored liquid made like coconut milk but with less water; it is creamier and thicker than coconut milk. The thick, fatty portion that separates and rises to the top of canned or frozen coconut milk is the cream. Do not substitute cream of coconut for true coconut cream.

Cream of coconut is a canned commercial product consisting of thick, sweetened coconut-flavored liquid; used for baking and beverages.

* Macadamias—Although commercially significant in Hawaii, macadamias are actually native to Australia. This small round nut is creamy white with a sweet, rich flavor and high fat content. Its shell is extremely hard and must be removed by machine, so the macadamia is always sold shelled. Its flavor blends well with fruit, coconut, and white and dark chocolate.

* Pecans—Native to the Mississippi River Valley, pecans are perhaps the most popular nuts in America. Their flavor is rich with a maple like taste and appears most often in breads, sweets, pastries, and cheesecake crusts. They are available whole in the shell or in various standard sizes and grades of pieces.

* Pistachios—Although native to central Asia, where they have been cultivated for more than three thousand years, California now produces most of the pistachios marketed in this country. Pistachios are unique for the green color of their meat. When ripe, the shell opens naturally at one end, aptly referred to as "smiling," which make shelling the nuts quite easy. Red pistachios are dyed, not natural. Pistachios are sold whole, shelled or unshelled, and are used in a variety of baked goods.

* Walnuts—Relatives of the pecan, walnuts are native to Asia, Europe, and North America. The black walnut, native to Appalachia, has a dark brown meat and a strong flavor. The English walnut, now grown primarily in California, has a milder flavor, is easier to shell, and is less expensive. Walnuts are more popular than pecans outside the United States. They are used in baked goods and are pressed for oil.

Salt

Salt is the most basic seasoning, and its use is universal. It preserves foods, heightens their flavors, and provides the distinctive taste of saltiness. The presence of salt can be tasted easily, but not smelled. Salt suppresses bitter flavors, making the sweet and sour ones more prominent. The flavor of salt will not evaporate or dissipate during cooking, so it should be added to food carefully, according to taste. Remember, you can always add more salt—but you can neither remove nor mask it if you have added too much.

* Sea salt—Sea salt, also known as *fleur de sel* or *sel gris*, is obtained, not surprisingly, by evaporating seawater. Unlike other table salts, sea salt contains additional mineral salts such as magnesium, calcium, and potassium, which give it a stronger, more complex flavor, and a grayish-brown color. The region where it is produced can also affect its flavor. For example, salt from the Mediterranean Sea will taste different than salt obtained from the Indian Ocean or the English Channel. Sea salt is considerably more expensive than other table salts and is often reserved for finishing a dish or used as a condiment.

* Kosher salt—Kosher salt has large, irregular crystals and it is used in the "Koshering" or curing of meats. It is purified rock salt that contains no iodine or additives. It can be substituted for common kitchen salt.

Spices

Spices are aromatic seasonings derived from the bark, roots, seeds, buds, or berries of plants and trees.

* All spice—Also known as Jamaican pepper, allspice is the dried berry of a tree that flourishes in Jamaica, and one of the few spices grown exclusively in the New World. Allspice is available whole, in berries that look like large, rough, brown peppercorns, or ground. Ground allspice is not a mixture of spices, although it does taste like a blend of cinnamon, cloves, and nutmeg. Allspice is now used throughout the world, in everything from cakes to curries, and is often included in peppercorn blends.

* Cardamom—One of the most expensive spices, second only to saffron in cost, cardamom seeds are encased in 1/4 inch long light green or brown pods. Cardamom is highly aromatic. Its flavor, lemony with notes of camphor, is quite strong and is used in both sweet and savory dishes. Cardamom is widely used in Indian and Middle Eastern cuisines, where it is also used to flavor coffee. Scandinavians use cardamom to flavor breads and pastries. Ground cardamom loses its flavor rapidly and is easily adulterated, so it is best to purchase the seeds whole and grind your own as needed.

* Cinnamon—Along with its cousin *cassia*, cinnamon is among the oldest known spices. Cinnamon's use is recorded in China as early as 2,500 BC, and the Far East still produces most of these products. Both cinnamon and cassia come from the bark of small evergreen trees, peeled from branches in thin layers and dried in the sun. High quality cinnamon should be pale brown and thin, rolled up like paper into stick known as quills. Cassia is coarser and has a stronger, less subtle flavor than cinnamon. Consequently, it is cheaper than true cinnamon. Cinnamon is usually purchased ground because it is difficult to grind. Cinnamon sticks are used when long cooking times allow for sufficient flavor to be extracted. Cinnamon's flavor is most often associated with pastries and sweets. Labeling laws do not require the packages distinguish between cassia and cinnamon, so most of what is sold as cinnamon in the United States is actually cassia, blended for consistent flavor and aroma.

* Cloves—The unopened buds of evergreen trees, cloves flourish in muggy tropical regions. Dried whole cloves have hard, sharp prongs that can be pushed into other foods, such as onions or fruit, in order to provide flavor. Cloves are extremely pungent, with a sweet,

astringent aroma. A small amount provides a great deal of flavor. Cloves used in desserts and meat dishes, preserves, and liquors. They may be purchased whole or ground.

* Ginger—A well known spice obtained from the root of a tall, flowering tropical plant. Fresh ginger root is known as a "hand" because it looks vaguely like a group of knobby fingers. Its flavor is fiery but sweet, with notes of lemon and rosemary. Fresh ginger is widely available and is used in Indian and Asian cuisines. Ginger is also available peeled and pickled in vinegar, candied in sugar, or preserved in alcohol or syrup. Dried, ground ginger is a fine yellow powder widely used in pastries. Its flavor is spicier than and not as sweet as fresh ginger.

* Nutmeg—Drying and opening the yellow plum-like fruit of a large tropical evergreen will reveal the seed known as nutmeg. The seed is surrounded by a bright red lacy coating or *aril*—also known as the spice mace. Whole nutmegs are oval and look rather like a piece of smooth wood. The flavor and aroma of nutmeg is strong and sweet, and a small quantity provides a great deal of flavor. Nutmeg should be grated directly into a dish as needed; once grated, flavor loss is rapid. Nutmeg is used in many European cuisines, mainly in pastries and sweets, but it is also important in meat and savory dishes. Mace is an expensive spice, with a flavor similar to nutmeg but more refined. It is almost always purchased ground and retains its flavor longer than other ground spices. Mace is used primarily in pastry items.

Sugar

Sugar is the most common and probably the first ingredient people think of when they think of desserts. Sugar and other sweeteners serve several purposes in the baking process. They provide sweetness, flavor and color, tenderize products by weakening gluten strands, provide food for yeasts, serve as a preservative, and act as a creaming or foaming agent to assist with leavening.

* Turbinado Sugar—Turbinado sugar, sometimes called demerara sugar, is the closest consumable product to *raw sugar*. It is partially refined, light brown in color, with coarse crystals and a caramel flavor. Because of its high and variable moisture content, turbinado sugar is not recommended as a substitute for granulated or brown sugar.

✳ Granulated Sugar—This is the all-purpose sugar used throughout the kitchen. The crystals are a fine, uniform size suitable for a variety of purposes.

✳ Brown Sugar—Brown sugar is simply regular refined sugar with some of the molasses returned to it. *Light brown sugar,* or *golden brown sugar,* contains approximately 3.5 percent molasses; *dark brown sugar* contains about 6.5 percent. Molasses adds moisture and a distinct flavor. Brown sugar can be substituted for refined sugar, measure for measure, in any formula where its flavor is desired. Because of the added moisture, brown sugar tends to lump, trapping air into its pockets. It should be measured by weight or, if measured by volume, it should be packed firmly into the measuring cup in order to remove any air pockets. Always store brown sugar in an airtight container to prevent it from drying or hardening.

✳ Superfine or Castor Sugar—Superfine sugar is granulated sugar with a smaller sized crystal. Also known as castor sugar, it can be produced by processing regular granulated sugar in a food processor for a few moments. Superfine sugar dissolves quickly in liquid and produces light and tender cakes.

✳ Powdered Sugar, also known as confectioners' sugar—Powdered sugar is made by grinding granulated sugar crystals through varying degrees of fine screens. Powdered sugar cannot be made in a food processor. It is widely available in three degrees of fineness: 10x is the finest and most common, 6x and 4x are progressively coarser. Because of powdered sugar's tendency to lump, 3 percent cornstarch is added to absorb moisture. Powdered sugar is most used in icings and glazes as for decorating baked products.

Vanilla

Vanilla is the most important and most frequently used flavoring in the pastry shop. The source of the flavor is the ripened, partially dried fruit of a tropical orchid. This fruit called a *vanilla bean* or *vanilla pod,* is readily available, but at a high price. In spite of their cost, vanilla beans are valued by pastry chefs for making the finest quality pastries and desserts sauces and fillings. Vanilla beans are purchased whole, individually, or by the pound. They should be soft and pliable, with a rich brown color and good aroma. The finest vanilla comes from Tahiti and Madagascar.

To use the vanilla bean, cut it open lengthwise with a paring knife. Scrape out the moist seeds with the knife tip and put them into the mixture being flavored. The seeds do not dissolve and will remain visible as small black or brown flecks. After all the seeds have been removed, the bean can be stored in a covered container with sugar to create vanilla sugar.

Vanilla beans should be stored in an airtight container in a cool, dark place. During storage, the beans may develop a white coating. This is not mold, but rather crystals of vanilla flavor known as *vanillin*. It should not be removed.

Pure *vanilla extract* is an easy and less expensive way to give baked product a true vanilla flavor. It is dark brown and aromatic, and comes in several strengths referred to as folds; the higher the number of folds, the stronger the flavor of the extract. Any products labeled "vanilla extract" must not contain artificial flavoring and must be at least 35 percent alcohol by volume. Vanilla extract should be stored at room temperature in a closed, opaque container. It should not be frozen. If a recipe calls for vanilla beans, there is no exact equivalent if you must substitute vanilla extract. This is because the strength of the flavor that is extracted from the bean depends on many factors, such as how long it was left in the liquid, whether or not it was split, and so on. However, a rule of thumb is to substitute 1/2 to 1 teaspoon of extract for each vanilla bean. Artificial or imitation vanilla flavoring is made with synthetic vanillin. Artificial flavoring is available in clear form, which is useful for white buttercream where the dark brown color of pure vanilla extract would be undesirable. Although inexpensive, artificial vanilla is, at best, weaker and less aromatic than pure extract. It can also impart a chemical or bitter taste to foods.

Wine & Spirits

Liquors, liqueurs, wines and *brandies* are frequently-used flavorings in baking. Liquors such as rum, bourbon, or whiskey can be used for their own distinct flavors or to blend with other flavors such as chocolate and coffee. Liqueurs are selected for their specific flavors; for example, kirsch for cherry, amaretto for almond, Kahlúa for coffee, crème de cassis for black currant, and crème de cacao for chocolate. They are used to either add or enhance flavors. Wine, both still and sparkling, is used as a flavoring or as a cooking medium (for example pears poached in red wine). Brandy, especially the classic orange flavored Grand Marnier, is another common bakeshop flavoring. Brandy compliments fruits and rounds off the flavor of custards and creams. When selecting an alcoholic beverage for baking, make the quality your first concern. Only high quality products will enhance the flavor and aroma of your baked goods. A simple rule of thumb is, if you won't drink it yourself, don't bake with it. The following liqueurs, wines, and spirits are used most often in this book.

Liquor—An alcoholic beverage made by distilling grains, vegetables, or other foods (includes rum, whiskey, and vodka).

* Dark Spiced Rum

* Dark Rum

* Ouzo (Greek liquor)

* Bourbon

* Vodka

* Irish Whiskey

Wine—An alcoholic beverage made from the fermented juice of grapes, can be sparkling (effervescent), still (non-effervescent), or fortified with additional alcohol.

* Cabernet Sauvignon

* Red Bordeaux

* Tawny Port

* Vouvray

* Mavrodaphne

* Cream Sherry

* White Riesling

* Semillon

Liqueur—Also known as a cordial, liqueur is a strong, sweet, syrupy alcoholic beverage made by mixing or redistilling neutral spirits with fruits, flowers, herbs, spices, or other flavorings.

* Grand Marnier

* Triple Sec

* Peachtree Schnapps

* Macadamia Nut Liqueur

* Crème de Cassis

* Cointreau

* Ouzo

* Káhlua

* Frangelico

Brandy—An alcoholic beverage made by distilling wine or the fermented mash of grapes or other fruits.

* Calvados

* Brandy

* Peach Brandy

* Cognac

In the Kitchen

Some Basic Equipment

In the average home kitchen, where we all do our cooking and baking, some of the necessary basic equipment is already on hand. It probably has a mixer of some kind, a set of mixing bowls, measuring cups and spoons, a whisk, a spatula, cake pans, and maybe a food processor. All of these are indispensable if you're going to get serious about making cheesecakes for your lavish holiday desserts. Having a well-equipped kitchen will transform your life making cheesecake preparation faster, more efficient, and will simplify the creation of a superb, enticing dessert. The following is a guide to the basic essential elements of the cheesecake-maker's kitchen.

When choosing your baking utensils and equipment, choose carefully, the better the quality, the longer it will last.

Bowls

A set of nested mixing bowls made of stainless steel, plastic, or tempered glass are easily stored and take up less space in your cupboards. The various sizes are useful for mixing fillings, melting chocolate, cooling compotes and cooked fruits quickly, and organizing prepared ingredients.

Citrus Zester

Zesters have a row of sharpened holes running across the top. When they are drawn firmly across a citrus fruit, they peel off long thin strands of zest. Many zesters have a canella knife on one side which removes a large V-shaped piece of zest. Both leave the bitter pith behind.

Cooling Rack

A wire mesh cooling rack simply lets air circulate underneath the cheesecake for rapid, even cooling.

Electric Mixers

There are essentially two types of electric mixers. The *hand-held mixer* is light, portable, and has a less powerful motor than its counterpart, the *stand mixer*. It is ideal for mixing or beating small amounts of fillings, creaming, whipping cream, and other quick jobs. Hand-held mixers are much less expensive than stand mixers.

The second type of electric mixer is the *stand mixer*, a heavy-duty version of the hand-held mixer. It is capable of handling both large and small quantities of mixtures, while leaving your hands free for other tasks. The stand mixer comes with three attachments, two of which will be used in the making of the cheesecakes in this book.

* The *wire whisk* incorporates maximum amounts of air into light mixtures, such as eggs, cream, and whipping cream.

* The *flat paddle* is mostly used for working with larger, firmer mixtures, such as creaming cream cheese and sugar, and making buttercream.

A relatively new brand-name product to the market, called the BeaterBlade, is an invaluable attachment for the stand mixer. The BeaterBlade looks like a conventional flat paddle beater, but with the addition of a flexible silicon edge that acts as a scraper for the mixing bowl. This flexible edge eliminates the need to stop the mixer to scrape down the side of the bowl. This is a timesaver when adding eggs to the cream cheese filling. It can be purchased online from http://www.beaterblade.com/ or from a specialty kitchen or cookware store.

Food Processor

The food processor has a motorized housing with a removable bowl and a metal S-shaped blade. Food processors usually come with several other cutting discs, but the S-shaped blade is the one that will be used most often when making your cheesecakes. The processor is ideal for chopping nuts and fruits, puréeing, and making crumb crusts.

Knives

A good set of knives are worth their weight in gold in the kitchen. It's worth the extra cost to purchase a set of high quality, high carbon, stainless steel knives. The knife should feel comfortable in the hand, designed to last, and stay sharp.

* A *chef's knife* with a 6- or 8-inch blade is the most versatile knife in the kitchen. It is ideal for chopping fruits, nuts, chocolate, and mincing zest.

* A *serrated bread knife* is a great knife for cutting citrus fruits, and can be used to slice your cheesecake.

* A *paring knife* with a 2- or 4-inch blade will serve well for peeling and coring fruit, mincing small quantities, and splitting and removing seeds from vanilla beans.

Measuring Cups

Both dry and liquid measuring cups will be needed for making cheesecakes.

* *Dry measuring cups* can be purchased in sets of 1/4, 1/3, 1/2, and 1 cup. Some sets also include a 2/3 and 3/4 cup. These sets are available in plastic and stainless steel.

* *Liquid measuring cups* differ from dry measuring cups in that they have an extended top, so liquids won't spill; and a pour spout, which makes pouring liquids easier. Look for measuring cups made out of heat resistant glass with easy-to-read markings. The cups are sold in 1, 2, and 4 cups capacities and are also available in plastic and metal.

Measuring Spoons

It is worthwhile to have two sets of measuring spoons for baking, because it is so handy. For dry ingredients, a narrow square set slides inside the bottles of spices. A set of narrow spoons includes 1/8, 1/4, 1/2, 3/4, 1 teaspoon, 1/2 tablespoon, and 1 tablespoon. The round set is perfect for liquids. Having both sets of measuring spoons means never having to worry about any dry ingredients sticking to a wet spoon or having to clean spoons while baking.

Pot Holders and Oven Mitts

Look for thick pads or gloves made out of heat resistant fabric or silicone. They protect the hands and forearms when removing hot items from the oven.

Roasting Pan

A heavy-duty roasting pan or broiler pan should be large enough to accommodate a 9- or 10-inch springform pan and hold enough water for a water bath used while baking the cheesecake. The roasting pan or broiler pan should have sturdy handles or a fat lip to make moving the water-filled pan in and out of the oven easier.

Saucepans

A saucepan should feel heavy in the hand, have a tight fitting lid, and a handle that stays cool and is comfortable to grip. Good quality pans are made of composite materials. An effective heat conducting metal, such as copper or aluminum, sandwiched between a non-reactive metal, like aluminum or stainless steel. Stainless interior saucepans have the added advantage of being shiny enough to make color changes easily visible—important when color change is an indicator of doneness.

Saucepans are available in a variety of sizes, ranging from small (1 to 1 1/2 quarts), to large (3 to 4 quarts). In the dessert kitchen, they're ideal for making fruit compote, caramel for buttercream, and topping sauces.

When a saucepan is coupled with a metal bowl, called a "bain-marie," it makes an ideal substitute for a double boiler.

Skillets

Quality skillet should have the same characteristics and construction as your saucepans. Skillets come in small (6 to 8 inches in diameter), medium (10 inches), and large (12 to 14 inches). Their shallow straight or sloping sides are ideal for reducing moisture in liquids in the quickest amount of time. In the baking kitchen, they are perfect for sautéing fruits and toasting nuts.

Spatulas

Spatulas come in many different sizes, shapes, and materials. The silicone spatula is the most practical spatula in the baking kitchen; it is flexible, heat resistant, stain resistant, and easily cleaned. Of all the available types of silicone spatulas, the scooped head style is a perfect match for making cheesecakes. It can be used to scrape down filling mixtures from the sides of mixing bowls, spooning fillings into springform pans, and spreading toppings on cheesecake. They're also great for stirring and folding.

> Icing spatulas are usually constructed of metal and come with both straight and offset blades. A small offset spatula is perfect for separating crumb crusts from the side of the springform pan and a large straight-bladed spatula for spreading toppings.

Springform Pans

Springform pans have removable sides that seal shut with a spring-loaded latch. Making a cheesecake in springform pans allows for easy removal of the pan's side. Springform pans come in several different sizes. (In this book, all of the recipes will use either a 9- or 10-inch pan.

Strainers

Strainers can be purchased in sets with coarse and fine meshes. They're useful for straining freshly squeezed citrus juice, fruit compote, and purées. Course strainers are useful for sifting dry ingredients together, for removing lumps from flour and sugar.

Whisks

Whisks incorporate air into ingredients and get the lumps out. They're ideal for blending dry ingredients for crumb crusts and stirring sauces until smooth. Balloon whisks consist of loops of stainless steel joined by a handle. They range from large ones for whipping to small ones for sauces. Flat whisks, which consist of a wire coiled around a loop, are useful of whisking in saucepans or containers without rounded bottoms.

Wooden spoons

Wooden spoons are useful for stirring, mixing, and beating as they do not conduct heat or scratch nonstick surfaces. Some spoons have flat edges and corners to help get into the sides of bowls and saucepans. Choose spoons made of hard, close grained wood for durability. Wooden spoons are inexpensive, so it is beneficial to keep an assortment of sizes on hand.

Tips and Techniques

Cheesecake preparation, like any other type of cooking, comes with its own particular set of techniques. Some techniques take several attempts before you'll gain confidence with them. The following are guidelines to the most commonly used cheesecake tips and techniques that will be used frequently throughout this book.

Getting familiar with the recipe

A recipe is a guide to cooking a specific dish, in this case, cheesecake. The following steps will be helpful to a successful outcome of your cheesecake.

Carefully read the recipe all the way through to develop a sense of what you are going to be baking. Then reread the recipe again, but this time take note of the ingredients used and the amounts needed, the techniques used, the order of events, and the timing. After this, you should have a fair idea of what the final outcome will look like and how to get there. Ingredients are listed in the order that they are used in the recipe.

After familiarizing yourself with the ingredients needed and methods to be used, the next thing to do is organize your ingredients and equipment. This is a crucial part of baking. Take items out of the refrigerator that need to be at room temperature. Peel, chop, and measure ingredients as directed in the recipe. Put them in bowls or containers in the order in which they will be used. Gather the equipment that will be needed to make the recipe by having ready all the small tools, bowls, pots and pans that will be needed for the recipe. Preheat the oven. All this preparation is referred to as *mise en place*, a French term that means "put in place." When everything is in its place, you can bake without complications.

For accuracy, measuring cups and spoons should be leveled with the back of a knife. For liquids measures, plastic and glass measuring cups with calibrations visible both inside and outside are the easiest to use.

Cooking times will vary depending on an individual oven and other factors such as the accuracy of the oven thermostat. It is a wise practice to use an oven thermometer to ensure the oven is maintaining the correct baking temperature.

Note: Baking is the most exacting form of cooking; even minor changes to a recipe can make a dramatic difference in the results. Therefore, it is suggested that substitutions not be made beyond what may be recommended in the recipe. Prepare the recipe at least once as written, and then experiment with your own variations.

Brown butter

Brown butter refers to butter that has been melted and cooked until golden brown. Browning the butter over medium-low heat cooks the milk solids in the butter, intensifying the butter flavor. This is a classic French technique that adds a full, nutty, buttery flavor to foods.

Buttercream

Buttercream toppings are light smooth mixtures of fat and sugar. They may also contain eggs to increase their smoothness or lightness. These popular icings are easily flavored to suit a variety of purposes.

There are many variations of buttercream recipes. The variety of buttercream to be used in this book is the French-style buttercream.

French buttercream is prepared by beating boiling syrup into beaten egg yolks and whipping it too a light foam. Soft butter is then whipped in. A variation of this style will be used in this book; instead of egg yolks, heavy cream and cream cheese will be used. The directions for preparing the buttercream toppings are included in the cheesecake recipes.

Creaming

Creaming is a mixing method in which softened fat and sugar are vigorously combined to incorporate air. Cream cheese is the most common fat that is used for cheesecake baking. In some instances other types of cheese will be used in combination with cream cheese in a recipe, such as cottage cheese, ricotta, or mascarpone cheese.

Make sure the cream cheese is at room temperature and soft so it creams properly with the sugar.

Beat the cream cheese and sugar in a large bowl until light and fluffy. This is easiest with an electric mixer.

The cream cheese and sugar should be smooth and fluffy and free of lumps.

Compotes

Compote is defined as cooked fruit, usually small fruits or cut fruit, served in its cooking liquid, usually sugar syrup. Cooking mediums range from light syrups to concentrated spiced caramel, honey, or liqueur mixtures.

The procedure for making specific compotes will be explained in detail in the recipes in which they are being used.

Flambéing

The principle of flambéing is very simple: the heating of spirits in a pan develops alcohol vapors that when brought into contact with an open flame, ignite. The excess alcohol is burned off, and through reduction of the spirits, the sauce is enhanced. When flambéing, you create a jet of flame that is pretty but could have unpleasant side effects. Always be sure when igniting the alcohol, hold your face back and the pan at arm's length. Also make sure to stay at a safe distance from all flammable materials. Turn off the heat and allow the flames to burn out.

Folding

Folding incorporates light, airy ingredients (such as whipped egg whites or whipped cream) into heavier ingredients (batter and filling) by gently moving them from the bottom of the bowl up over the top in a circular motion, usually with a rubber spatula.

Measuring dry ingredients

Accurately measuring ingredients is a crucial step in the baking process, too little or too much can change the outcome. To measure accurately, fill a measuring cup or measuring spoon with the ingredient and level off with a back of a knife.

Measuring liquids

Using a glass or plastic measuring cup with the measurements clearly marked on the side, set the cup on a flat surface and fill to the called for amount. After the liquid has settled, bend down and read the measurement at eye level for accuracy.

Melting chocolate

The most common method of melting chocolate is the use of a double boiler or a bain-marie*. The water in the lower container should not exceed 140°F and the upper container should not touch the water.

Chop or break the chocolate into approximately 1/2-inch pieces to ensure even melting.

Place the chopped chocolate in the upper container of the double boiler over gently simmering water. Add 1/4 cup of water. The water reduces the chances of the chocolate scorching or burning.

Stir until the chocolate is smooth, using a silicone spatula. The silicone spatula works well because it does not impart any flavors into the chocolate.

An important thing to remember when melting chocolate, the temperature of the chocolate should not exceed 120°F or there will be loss of flavor.

*Note: A bain-marie is a simple substitute for a double boiler in the event one is not available, simply place a metal bowl over a saucepan of simmering water and you have a make-shift double boiler.

Toasting nuts

Taking the extra step of toasting nuts in a recipe brings out their flavor and improves the quality of the cheesecake. Place the nuts in a thick-bottomed sauté pan over medium-high heat, shaking or stirring frequently, cooking until golden brown and slightly fragrant. Cooking times will vary depending on the kind of nuts and the size of the nuts that are being toasted. Times will vary from 3 to 5 minutes for sliced and slivered nuts to 12 to 15 minutes for whole and large nuts.

Vanilla bean seeding

Vanilla bean seeding is the process of removing the miniature seeds from the vanilla bean pod. Place the vanilla bean flat on a cutting board. Using a paring knife, slice the bean pod length-wise from the stem end to the opposite end.

Holding the stem end, using the same knife, scrape down the length of the split pod, removing the tiny, moist seeds.

Water baths

A water bath is a way of baking a cheesecake in the oven with a gentle moist heat. Cheesecake is custard at heart. It's delicate, so you want to bake it slowly and evenly without over browning the top.

The most effective way to do this is to use a water bath. Since water evaporates at the boiling point, the water bath will never get hotter than 212°F, no matter what the oven temperature. This means that the outer edge of the cheesecake won't bake faster than the center, which can cause it to crack.

When using a springform pan, check that the seal between the removable bottom and the side of pan is water tight. A layer of heavy aluminum foil on the outside around the bottom and the sides may be necessary to prevent leakage while baking the cheesecake.

Place the batter-filled springform pan into a roasting pan with 2- to 3-inch sides. There should be at least a 1/2 to 1 inch clearance between the side of the springform pan and the side of the roasting pan.

Place the pans into a preheated oven. Carefully pour boiling water, from a kettle, into the roasting pan so that the water level comes halfway up the side of the springform pan. Caution, the use of cold water for the water bath will retard the baking time.

Bake the cheesecake as directed. When the cheesecake is done, remove the springform pan from the water bath, and place it on a wire rack to cool.

Carefully remove the roasting pan from the oven and discard the water. Continue to follow the recipe directions for cooling and the removal of the side of the cake pan.

As was mentioned earlier, the seal between the removable bottom and the side of the springform pan should be watertight. A simple test can be performed at home or in a store if a new springform pan is being purchased, to check if the seal is watertight or if it will possibly leak water from the bath. Grasp the side of the pan with the thumb and forefinger of both hands. With the remaining fingers apply pressure to the bottom of the pan. If the bottom moves back and forth or pops out of the sealing groove, it will likely leak. The solution is to wrap two layers of heavy-duty aluminum foil around the bottom and sides of the springform pan to prevent leakage in the seal.

Cracking

"What is the most common problem that occurs to your homemade cheesecakes?" Inevitably, the home cheesecake baker's answer would most likely be "The top of my cheesecake cracked." This is not the end of the world—a cracked top will not affect the texture or taste of the cheesecake. However, the home cheesecake baker's quest to produce the perfect cheesecake with uncracked, lightly browned tops has become more of an ego thing than anything else. Cracks are a visual imperfection and are easily remedied; more importantly, easily avoided.

The following is a list of preventative measures to avoid ugly cracks from showing on the top of your cheesecake.

- Lightly grease the entire inside of the springform pan with butter. This helps the crust release from the side of the pan as it cools and shrinks.

- Avoid overbeating filling after eggs have been added. Over beating will add too much air into the mixture which gets trapped in between the egg molecules; as the filling is heated the air bubbles expand and escape to the surface causing cracks on the top of the cake.

- Baking the cheesecake at too high of a temperature or too long will cause the cake to crack. Baking at too high of a temperature causes the cheesecake to bake unevenly. The edges cook faster than the center and moisture evaporates too quickly causing cracks.

- Overcooking a cheesecake is the most frequent cause of cracking because they are deceptive when trying to figure out when they are done baking. When it's done baking, it never appears to be done. The cheesecake is done baking when the edges are firm and the center jiggles slightly when the pan is gently shaken.

- Sudden changes in temperature will also cause cracks in a cheesecake. The oven door should not be opened within the first 30 minutes of baking time. This will cause a sudden change in temperature and drafts, possibly resulting in a fallen cheesecake or cracks. Finally, never put a cooling cheesecake by an open window or air conditioner; it will also result in too rapid and uneven cooling—causing cracks.

- Baking your cheesecake in a water bath insulates the cake from high heat exposure and controls the rate at which the heat moves into the cheesecake, and also adds moisture to the oven's environment, preventing cracking.

- After your cheesecake has cooled for 30 minutes to 1 hour, running a small knife around the springform pan between its side and crust of the cheesecake will prevent the cake from cracking as it cools and shrinks.

- The last preventative measure to avoid cracks in the top of your cheesecake is to simply add 1 to 3 tablespoons of cornstarch to the cream cheese along with the sugar.

In the event that your cheesecake does crack, the cure is very simple: use compotes, sauces, buttercream, and fresh fruits to easily cover the cracks.

Freezing Cheesecakes

Yes, your cheesecake can be frozen for up to 1 month (any longer will diminish the quality of the cheesecake). Place the fully-cooled cheesecake, uncovered, in the freezer for 1 hour. After 1 hour remove the cheesecake from the freezer and carefully wrap it in plastic wrap, then wrap it in heavy-duty aluminum foil or place it in a large freezer bag. Label and date the wrapped cheesecake and return to the freezer.

When ready to use the cheesecake, transfer it from the freezer to the refrigerator and thaw overnight. When the cheesecake is partially thawed, remove the springform pan bottom and transfer to a serving plate. Finish cheesecake with desired topping and serve.

Cheesecake

*T*hese icons of indulgence are sure to make holiday guests scrape their plates and not leave a crumb. No other dessert catapults from basic to highbrow so gracefully. No other dessert flatters other flavors so gallantly. And no other dessert offers something for everyone the way cheesecake does. So let's get baking.

Thanksgiving

Thanksgiving is the traditional start of the holiday season, it's all about food and family traditions, so trying something new can be risky.

Dessert can be an exception a slice of creamy cheesecake makes an elegant alternative to apple or pumpkin pie. It's not hard to "sell" guests on cheesecake. And since it can be made a day or so ahead, it's perfect for the hectic holiday schedule.

Thanksgiving Cheesecake Suggestions

Pumpkin Mousse Cheesecake with Gingersnap-Pecan Crust and Caramel Buttercream with Bacon and Sea Salt

Crust

1 1/2 c.   purchased gingersnap cookies, finely ground

1 c.   pecans, finely chopped

1/4 c.   light brown sugar, packed

2 tbsp.   crystallized ginger, chopped (optional)

4 tbsp.   unsalted butter, melted

Preheat oven to 350°F.

Lightly butter a 9-inch springform pan with 2 3/4-inch high sides; wrap outside of pan with 2 layers of heavy-duty foil and set aside.

In a food processor, add gingersnap cookies and pecans and pulse until finely ground.

Transfer mixture to a medium-size bowl and add the brown sugar and ginger, combining thoroughly. Add the melted butter and combine with a fork until crust mixture is evenly moistened and sticks together when lightly pressed. Press the mixture onto bottom and 1 to 1 1/2 inches up the side of the pan.

Bake the crust until set and lightly browned on the edges for about 10 to 12 minutes. Cool on a wire rack.

Filling

8 oz.	hickory smoked bacon, diced
4	8 oz. packages cream cheese, room temperature
2 c.	granulated sugar
1	15 oz. can pure pumpkin purée
5	large eggs, room temperature
4 tbsp.	all-purpose flour
1 tsp.	ground cinnamon
1 tsp.	ground ginger
1/4 tsp.	ground nutmeg
1/4 tsp.	ground allspice
1/4 tsp.	kosher salt
2 tsp.	pure vanilla extract

Cook bacon in a sauté pan over medium heat until crisp; drain on paper towel-lined plate and set aside. Reserve 2 tablespoons of the bacon drippings.

Using an electric mixer fitted with the paddle attachment, beat the cream cheese and sugar for about 3 to 5 minutes until smooth and fluffy. Beat in the pumpkin until thoroughly combined.

On low speed, add eggs one at a time, and beat until just blended, scraping down the side of the bowl after each addition. Add flour, spices and salt; beat just to blend. Beat in the vanilla and bacon drippings until just blended making sure not to overmix after the eggs have been added. Pour into springform pan.

Place the springform pan in a large roasting pan with 2- to 3-inch high sides, and pour in enough boiling water to come halfway up outside of cake pan.

Bake cheesecake for about 1 hour and 20 minutes, until edge is set and begins to crack and center moves slightly when the pan is gently shaken. Remove springform pan from oven to a wire rack, remove foil, and cool for 1 hour. After 1 hour, cut around edge of pan with a small knife or metal spatula to loosen crust from side of the pan. Cool to room temperature for about 4 hours. Chill uncovered in cake pan for 8 hours or overnight.

Buttercream

1 c.	light brown sugar, packed
3 tbsp.	water
	Pinch of kosher salt
1/4 c.	heavy cream
4 tbsp.	unsalted butter, cubed
2 oz.	cream cheese, cut into 1/2-inch cubes
	coarse sea salt

Combine brown sugar, water, and salt in a medium-size saucepan and boil over high heat about 5 minutes, gently swirling occasionally to prevent scorching. Whisk in the cream and butter pieces (mixture will bubble furiously; keep whisking). Boil for 2 more minutes.

Transfer caramel to the bowl of a stand mixer and whip on high speed for 8 to 10 minutes until side of bowl is cool to the touch and caramel is thick, scraping down side of the bowl as needed. Add the cream cheese 1 cube at a time and beat until buttercream is smooth. Evenly spread the buttercream topping onto the chilled cheesecake; sprinkle top with bacon and sea salt and chill 1 to 2 hours before serving. Enjoy!

Chef's tip: Cheesecake tends to be on the heavy side and will be easier to cut using a knife dipped in hot water and dried in between cutting slices.

Indian Pudding Cheesecake
with black walnut crust and rich brandy sauce

Recipe inspired by Jasper White's *Cooking from New England*, Indian pudding (page 305).

Indian Pudding

2 1/2 tbsp. unsalted butter, divided

3 c.   milk

1/3 c.   yellow cornmeal

1/3 c.   molasses

1/3 c.   maple syrup

1/4 tsp.   kosher salt

1/4 tsp.   ground cinnamon

1/2 tsp.   ground ginger

1   egg, beaten

1 c.   cold milk

Preheat the oven to 300°F.

Grease a 1 1/2 quart baking dish with 1 tablespoon butter; set aside.

Heat milk in a saucepan until it is close to a boil. Add the cornmeal and reduce heat to low. Stir for 5 minutes or until mixture thickens. Remove the saucepan from the heat, and add the remaining butter, molasses, maple syrup, salt, cinnamon, ginger, and egg. Stir to combine thoroughly.

Pour batter into the buttered baking dish.

Place the baking dish into the oven and bake for 30 minutes. Pour the cold milk over the pudding and return to the oven. Cook for 1 hour and 30 minutes more or until the top is brown and crisp. Transfer to a wire rack and cool.

Note: Pudding can be made 1 to 3 days ahead, cover and refrigerate.

Crust

1 c.   black walnuts, toasted, and finely chopped

1/2 c.   graham cracker crumbs

1/4 c.   granulated sugar

5 tbsp.   unsalted butter, melted

Increase oven temperature to 350°F.

Lightly butter a 9-inch springform pan with 2 3/4-inch high sides and wrap the outside of pan with 2 layers of heavy-duty foil; set aside.

In a medium-size bowl, combine the black walnuts, graham cracker crumbs, and sugar; with a fork; mix the ingredients thoroughly. Add butter and blend until mixture is evenly moistened and crumbs stick together when lightly pressed. Press the crumb mixture over the bottom and 1 to 1 1/2 inches up the side of the cake pan; set aside.

Filling

4	8 oz. packages cream cheese, room temperature
2 c.	granulated sugar
2 c.	reserved Indian pudding
5	large eggs, room temperature
4 tbsp.	all-purpose flour
1/4 tsp.	kosher salt
2 tbsp.	pure vanilla extract

In the bowl of a stand mixer fitted with the paddle attachment, beat cream cheese and sugar on medium-high speed for about 3 to 5 minutes until smooth. Beat in Indian pudding until thoroughly blended in. Turn mixer to low speed. Add eggs one at a time and beat until just blended, scraping down the sides of the bowl after each addition. Add the flour, salt, and vanilla; and beat until just blended making sure not to overmix after the eggs have been added. Pour filling over crust.

Place the springform pan in a large roasting pan with 3-inch high sides, and pour enough boiling water into the roasting pan to come half way up the side of the cake pan.

Bake cheesecake for 1 hour and 20 minutes or until edge is set and center wiggles when the pan is gently shaken. Remove springform pan from the oven and transfer to a wire rack and cool for 1 hour.

Run a small knife or metal spatula around the rim to loosen the crust from the side of the pan. Cool to room temperature for about 4 hours. Chill for 8 hours or overnight in the pan.

Brandy Sauce

2 c.	heavy cream
4	large eggs yolks
1/2 c.	granulated sugar
3 tbsp.	brandy
1/4 c.	black walnuts, coarsely chopped

In a heavy-bottomed saucepan bring cream to a boil. In a separate bowl, whisk the egg yolks and the sugar together until smooth and creamy. Slowly pour the hot cream into the egg yolks and sugar mixture, constantly stirring. Return sauce to the saucepan and stir over low heat for 5 to 6 minutes, until slightly thickened. Do not boil. Stir in brandy just before serving.

Maple Buttercream (optional topping)

1 c.	granulated sugar
3 tbsp.	water
	Pinch of kosher salt
1/4 c.	heavy cream
4 tbsp.	unsalted butter, cubed
2 oz.	cream cheese, cut into 1-inch cubes
4 tbsp.	pure maple syrup

Boil the sugar, water, and pinch of salt in a medium-size saucepan over high heat for about 5 minutes; gently swirling occasionally to prevent scorching. Whisk in the cream and butter pieces (mixture will bubble furiously; keep whisking). Boil for 2 minutes more.

Transfer the sugar syrup to the bowl of a stand mixer; whip on high-speed for about 8 to 10 minutes until the side of the bowl is cool to the touch and syrup is thick, scraping down sides of the bowl as needed. Add cream cheese 1 cube at a time until buttercream is smooth. Stir in maple syrup and blend thoroughly. Spread buttercream over the top of chilled cheesecake, and keep chilled until just before serving. Serve and enjoy!

Caramelized Apple-Ginger Cheesecake with Gingerbread-Pecan Crust and Apple Topping

Crust

1 1/2 c.   purchased gingersnap cookies, finely ground

1/2 c.   pecans, finely chopped, plus additional pecan halves for garnish

1/4 c.   brown sugar, packed

4 tbsp.   unsalted butter, melted

Preheat oven to 350°F

Lightly butter a 9-inch springform pan with 2 3/4-inch high sides, and wrap the outside of the pan with 2 layers of heavy-duty foil.

In a food processor, grind the gingersnap cookies and pecans; transfer crumbs to a medium-size bowl. Add brown sugar and combine thoroughly. Add melted butter and blend with a fork until crumbs are evenly moistened and stick together when lightly pressed.

Press crumb mixture over bottom and 1 to 1 1/2 inches up the side of the prepared pan. Bake the crust for 10 to 12 minutes or until set and lightly browned. Remove pan from the oven and cool completely on a wire rack.

Caramelized Apples

4 to 5	Honeycrisp apples, peeled, cored, and sliced (1/4-inch thick)
1/3 c.	brown sugar, packed
4 tbsp.	unsalted butter
1/2 tsp.	fresh gingerroot, grated
	Pinch of kosher salt
1/2 c.	brandy

In a large skillet over medium heat, heat the brown sugar and butter, stirring and swirling, until the mixture is smooth and turns into a light amber color. Add the apples, ginger, and salt, turning the apples occasionally, and continue to simmer until the apples are tender and coated with caramel.

Drain excess liquid from the skillet. Add the brandy to the skillet, holding the pan at arms length, slightly tilt the pan and ignite the brandy to flambé the apples. Remove the pan from the heat, allowing flames to burn out, and cool slightly.

Filling

4	8 oz. packages cream cheese, room temperature
1 1/4 c.	granulated sugar
3 tbsp.	all-purpose flour
1 1/2 tsp.	pure vanilla extract
4	eggs, room temperature
1/2 tsp.	fresh lemon juice

1/2 c.   sour cream

2 tbsp.   brandy

In the large bowl of a stand mixer fitted with the paddle attachment, beat the cream cheese until smooth for about 3 to 5 minutes. On low speed add the sugar, flour, and vanilla and continue to beat for an additional 2 to 3 minutes on low speed. Add the eggs one at a time, scraping down the side of the bowl after each addition, and mix until just blended. Add the lemon juice, sour cream, and brandy and beat until just blended, making sure not to overmix after the eggs have been added.

Pour half of the filling over the crust in the prepared pan and spread evenly. Arrange half of the caramelized apples in a circular pattern over the filling. Pour the remaining half of the filling over the apples. Tap the pan on the countertop a few times to release any trapped air bubbles in the filling. Place the springform pan into a large roasting pan with 3-inch high sides and pour in enough boiling water to come halfway up the outside of the springform pan.

Bake for 1 hour to 1 hour and 15 minutes or until edge is set and center wobbles when the pan is gently shaken.

Remove the cheesecake from the water bath and transfer to a wire rack; remove foil and cool for 1 hour. Run a small knife or metal spatula around the rim of the pan to loosen the crust from side of the pan. Continue to cool the cheesecake to room temperature for about 3 to 4 hours.

Cover top of cheesecake with remaining apples in a circular pattern as before with the filling. Decorate with pecan halves and chill for 8 hours, or overnight, before serving. Enjoy!

Brandy Caramel Sauce *(optional topping)*

1/2 c.	granulated sugar
3 tbsp.	brandy, plus 2 tsp.
3 tbsp.	water
1 tsp.	fresh lemon juice
1/4 c.	heavy cream
1 tsp.	pure vanilla extract
1/4 c.	pecans, coarsely broken

Combine sugar, 3 tablespoons brandy, water, and lemon juice in a medium saucepan, over medium-high heat, and cook for 2 minutes or until sugar is dissolved, stirring constantly. Bring mixture to a boil; reduce heat to medium and cook, without stirring, 10 minutes longer or until syrup is golden in color. Remove the saucepan from the heat. Whisk in the cream, stirring constantly (mixture will bubble vigorously). Cool caramel sauce slightly. Stir in remaining 2 teaspoons of brandy, vanilla, and pecans. Top sliced cheesecake with sauce and serve. Enjoy!

Decadent Chocolate-Cranberry Cheesecake with Chocolate Wafer Crust and Cranberry Filling with Simmered Orange Topping

Cranberry Compote

1	12 oz. package fresh cranberries
3/4 c.	granulated sugar
2/3 c.	cranberry juice
	Zest of 1 orange, minced
1/4 c.	triple sec

In a medium-size saucepan, combine cranberries, sugar, and cranberry juice; bring mixture to a boil over medium-high heat, stirring until sugar dissolves. Reduce heat to low and gently simmer uncovered for 3 to 4 minutes or until cranberries pop. Add orange zest and triple sec and cook for an additional 3 to 5 minutes or until compote thickens, stirring occasionally. Set compote aside to cool.

When the compote has cooled slightly, strain 1 1/2 cups through a fine mesh strainer. Transfer strained compote to separate bowl and continue to cool. Strained cranberry compote will be used in the filling.

Chef's note: cranberry compote can be made up to 3 days ahead, cover and refrigerate.

Crust

1 1/2 c.	purchased chocolate wafer cookies, finely crushed
1/4 c.	walnuts, chopped
1 tbsp.	all-purpose flour
6 tbsp.	unsalted butter, melted

Preheat oven to 350°F.

Lightly butter a 9-inch springform pan with 2 3/4 -inch high sides. Wrap the outside of pan with 2 layers of heavy-duty foil.

In a medium-size bowl, mix together chocolate wafer crumbs, flour, and walnuts; with a fork combine thoroughly. Stir in butter and blend until mixture is evenly moistened and crumbs stick together when pressed. Press crumb mixture into the bottom and 1 to 1 1/2 inches up the side of the springform pan and set aside.

Filling

3	8 oz. package cream cheese, room temperature
1 c.	granulated sugar
1/4 tsp.	kosher salt
1	vanilla bean, seeded

3 tbsp.	all-purpose flour
3	large eggs, room temperature
1/4 c.	sour cream
8 oz.	semisweet chocolate, melted and cooled

In a double boiler or bain-marie, over gently simmering water, add the chopped chocolate and 1/4 cup water and stir until chocolate is melted and smooth. Remove melted chocolate from heat and cool slightly.

In the bowl of an electric mixer fitted with the paddle attachment, beat the cream cheese on medium-high speed for 3 to 5 minutes or until creamy and smooth. Gradually add sugar, salt, vanilla bean seeds, and flour; mix for an additional 2 to 3 minutes. Reduce the mixer speed to low and beat in the eggs one at a time, until just blended, scraping down the sides of the bowl after each addition. Beat in sour cream until combined. Divide filling in half.

Stir the melted chocolate into remaining half of filling in the mixing bowl and mix until evenly blended. Pour the chocolate filling over the crust in the prepared pan spreading evenly.

Carefully spoon strained cranberry compote, in an even layer, over the chocolate filling. Spoon the remaining filling over the cranberry compote, again in an even layer.

Place springform pan in a roasting pan with 2- to 3-inch high sides and carefully pour enough boiling water to come up halfway up the outside of the springform pan.

Bake the cheesecake for 1 hour to 1 hour and 15 minutes or until outer edge appears set and center jiggles when pan is gently shaken.

Transfer cake pan to wire rack, remove foil, and cool for 1 hour. Using a small knife, loosen crust from side of the pan and continue to cool to room temperature for about 4 hours.

Simmered oranges

4	oranges, cut into 1/4-inch slices, discard seeds
1 1/2 c.	granulated sugar
1/4 c.	water
1/4 c.	orange juice
1/4 c.	lemon juice

In a 12-inch skillet, combine sugar, water, orange juice, and lemon juice. Bring to a boil over medium heat, stirring until sugar is dissolved. Reduce heat to simmer and cook uncovered for about 10 minutes or until mixture is syrupy. Add orange slices and simmer, uncovered for about 3 minutes or until oranges are tender, turning occasionally; cool.

Shingle simmered oranges around outer edge of cheesecake. Next, place a 4-inch container in the center of the cheesecake and spoon remaining compote around the container forming a ring. Carefully remove the container and fill in center of cheesecake with oranges, the same as the outer edge. Brush syrup from oranges over the oranges; cover and chill for 8 hours or overnight before serving. Serve and enjoy!

Fresh Peach Cheesecake with Gingersnap-Hazelnut Crust and Peach Compote Topping

Crust

2 c.   purchased gingersnap cookies, finely ground

1/2 c.   hazelnuts, toasted and finely chopped

1/4 c.   brown sugar, packed

4 tbsp.   unsalted butter, melted

Preheat oven to 350°F.

Lightly butter a 9-inch springform pan with 2 3/4-inch high sides and wrap with 2 layers of heavy-duty foil.

In a food processor, add gingersnap cookies and hazelnuts; pulse until finely ground. Transfer crumbs to a medium-size bowl, add brown sugar and combine thoroughly with a fork. Add the melted butter and mix until crumbs are evenly moist and stick together when lightly pressed. Press crumb mixture over bottom and 1 to 1 1/2 inches up the side of the springform pan.

Bake the crust for 10 to 12 minutes or until set and lightly browned. Remove crust from the oven to a wire rack and cool completely.

Chef's tip: To remove the skins from the hazelnuts, roast nuts on a baking sheet in a 350°F oven for 8 minutes. Remove from oven and rub them in a soft towel to loosen the skins.

Peach Compote

2 1/2 lbs.	fresh ripe peaches, peeled, pitted and cut into 1/8" wedges.
4 tbsp.	unsalted butter
2/3 c.	brown sugar, packed
1/2	lime, thinly sliced and seeded
1	cinnamon stick
3	whole cloves
1/4 tsp.	kosher salt
1	star anise
6	whole black peppercorns
1/2 c.	peach brandy

In a large skillet, over medium-high heat, melt the butter. Add the brown sugar, lime, cinnamon stick, cloves, salt, star anise, and black peppercorns and allow the mixture to caramelize for about 5 to 8 minutes. Add the peaches and cook for 3 to 5 minutes or until the peaches are tender and well coated with sauce.

Remove the skillet from heat and discard lime, cinnamon stick, cloves, anise and peppercorns. Add the brandy and ignite to flambé the peaches. (Note: See Tips and Techniques for flambéing procedure). Remove pan from heat and allow flames to burn out.

Drain peaches over a bowl and set aside to cool.

Filling

4	8 oz. packages cream cheese, room temperature
1 c.	granulated sugar
3 tbsp.	flour
4	large eggs, room temperature
1/2 c.	sour cream
	Pinch of kosher salt
1/2 tsp.	pure vanilla extract
1 tbsp.	peach brandy

In the bowl of a stand mixer fitted with the paddle attachment, beat the cream cheese on medium-high speed until smooth. Gradually add sugar and flour, and beat until fluffy for about 3 to 5 minutes. Reduce mixer speed to low; add eggs one at a time and beat until just blended, scraping down the sides of the bowl after each addition. Add sour cream, salt, vanilla extract and brandy, mix until just blended. Caution, do not overmix filling after eggs have been added, it may cause cake to crack while baking.

Spoon half the filling over the crust. Carefully spoon half of drained peaches over filling, spacing apart evenly. Pour the remaining filling into cake pan and spread evenly.

Place springform pan in a large roasting pan with 2- to 3-inch high sides; pour enough boiling water into pan to come halfway up the outside of the springform pan.

Bake the cheesecake for 1 hour and 5 minutes or until the edge is set and center moves slightly when the pan is gently shaken.

Remove pan from the oven and move to a wire rack, remove foil, and cool for 1 hour. Loosen crust from the side of the springform pan with a small knife and continue to cool to room temperature for about 4 hours.

Arrange remaining peaches in a circular pattern covering entire top of cheesecake. Cover and refrigerate for 8 hours or overnight. Tightly cover and refrigerate reserved compote sauce.

Drizzle sauce over sliced cheesecake before serving. Enjoy!

Chef's tip: To peel peaches make a small X on the bottom of each peach and place them in a large bowl. Pour boiling water over the peaches and let stand for 30 to 40 seconds. Removed blanched peaches from the bowl and transfer to a strainer and cool under cold water or plunge peaches into an ice bath. The second and easiest way to peel peaches is to use of a serrated peeler, available at kitchen supply houses and many supermarkets.

White Chocolate Cheesecake with Cashew Crust and Cranberry-Pomegranate Sauce

Crust

1 c.   cashews, very finely chopped

1 c.   graham cracker crumbs

1/2 c.   granulated sugar

8 tbsp.   unsalted butter, melted

Preheat oven to 350°F.

Lightly butter a 10-inch springform pan with 2 3/4-inch high sides. Wrap the outside of pan with 2 layers of heavy-duty foil.

In a medium-size bowl, combine chopped cashews, graham crackers, and sugar; stir in butter and mix until mixture is evenly moistened. Press crumb mixture over the bottom of pan and 1 to 1 1/2 inches up the side of pan and set aside.

Note: Toasted black walnuts can be used as an option for cashews.

Cranberry-Pomegranate Sauce

1 c.	pomegranate juice
3/4 c.	granulated sugar
1 tbsp.	orange zest, minced
1/2 tsp.	ground cardamom
1	12 oz. bag fresh or frozen cranberries

In a medium-size saucepan, over medium heat, bring to a boil pomegranate juice, sugar, orange zest, and cardamom; stirring until sugar dissolves. Reduce heat to low, add cranberries and simmer for 10 to 12 minutes or until berries burst and sauce thickens.

Remove saucepan from heat and cool to room temperature, then chill sauce for 2 hours. Sauce can be made up to 2 days ahead, covered and refrigerated.

Filling

1 lb.	good quality white chocolate (Lindt or Baker's), finely chopped
4	8 oz. packages cream cheese, room temperature
1 c.	granulated sugar
1/4 tsp.	kosher salt
4	large eggs, room temperature
1 c.	sour cream
1/2 c.	heavy cream

2 tbsp.   pure vanilla extract

In a double boiler or bain-marie, over slow simmering water, add to top container 1/4 cup of water and chopped chocolate and melt until smooth, stirring occasionally. Remove from over water and cool chocolate to lukewarm.

In the large bowl of an electric mixer fitted with the paddle attachment, beat cream cheese on medium-high speed until creamy and smooth for about 3 to 5 minutes. Gradually add sugar, then salt and beat until fluffy, for 2 to 3 minutes more, scraping down sides of bowl occasionally. Reduce mixer speed to low, add eggs one at a time and beat again until just blended; scraping down sides of bowl after each addition. Add the sour cream, heavy cream, and vanilla; mix until just blended. Do not overmix.

Pour filling over crust and spread evenly over bottom of prepared pan. Place springform pan in a large roasting pan with 2- to 3-inch sides; pour enough boiling water into pan to come halfway up the outside of the springform pan.

Bake the cake for 1 hour and 40 minutes or until the top begins to brown lightly and center moves slightly when pan is gently shaken.

Remove cake pan from oven and move to wire rack, remove foil, and cool for 1 hour. Loosen crust from side of springform pan with a small knife and continue to cool to room temperature for about 4 hours.

Cover top of the cheesecake with cranberry-pomegranate sauce and spread evenly over cake. Cover and refrigerate for 8 hours or overnight.

Chef's note: Cheesecake can be made 2 days ahead. Cover and keep refrigerated. Serve and enjoy!

Honey-Lemon Cranberry Sauce with Rosemary
(optional topping #1)

1/2 c.	wildflower honey
1/2 c.	granulated sugar
1/2 c.	fresh lemon juice
1/4 c.	water
2	sprigs fresh rosemary
	Pinch of kosher salt
1	12 oz. bag fresh cranberries

In a medium-size saucepan bring to a boil honey, sugar, lemon juice, water, rosemary, and salt over medium-high heat. Reduce heat to a slow simmer, add cranberries and cook for 8 to 10 minutes or until berries pop and sauce thickens; remove rosemary sprigs. Chill at least 2 to 3 hours before topping cheesecake.

Sauce can be made up to 2 to 3 days ahead, covered and refrigerated.

Cranberry-Cherry Sauce with Lime and Ginger
(optional topping #2)

1 c.	granulated sugar
3/4 c.	water
1/2 c.	tart cherries, dried
1/4 c.	fresh lime juice
2 tbsp.	crystallized ginger, chopped

Pinch of kosher salt

1   12 oz. bag fresh cranberries

In a medium-size saucepan bring to a boil sugar, water, cherries, lime juice, ginger, and salt over medium-high heat, stirring until sugar dissolves. Reduce heat to a slow simmer, add cranberries and cook for 8 to 10 minutes or until berries pop and sauce thickens. Chill at least 2 to 3 hours before topping cheesecake.

Sauce can be made up to 2 to 3 days ahead, covered and refrigerated.

Chef's tip: leftover sauces can be used as side dishes with leftovers from dinner or as a topping for ice cream or frozen yogurt.

Red Currant Cheesecake with Spiced Currant Compote and Toasted Almonds

Crust

1 1/2 c.   graham cracker, crumbs

3/4 c.   toasted sliced almonds, finely chopped, divided

1/4 c.   light brown sugar

1/4 tsp.   ground cinnamon

Pinch kosher salt

6 tbsp.   unsalted butter, melted

Preheat oven to 350°F.

Lightly butter a 9-inch springform pan with 2 3/4-inch high sides and wrap outside of pan with 2 layers of heavy-duty foil.

In a medium-size bowl combine graham crumbs, 1/2 cup toasted almonds, brown sugar, cinnamon, and salt. Add butter and mix with a fork until mixture is evenly moistened and sticks together when lightly pressed. Press crumb mixture over bottom of pan and 1 to 1 1/2 inches up the side of the cake pan.

Bake crust for 10 to 12 minutes or until set and golden. Cool crust completely on a wire rack and set aside.

Currant Compote

1 1/2 lb.	fresh red currants
1 c.	granulated sugar
1/4 c.	water
1/2 tsp.	ground cinnamon
1/4 tsp.	allspice
1/4 tsp.	ground cloves
2 tbsp.	cream sherry

Chef's Note: White currants may be used instead of red currants.

In a medium-size saucepan, over medium-high heat, combine currants, sugar, and water and bring to a boil, stirring occasionally. Reduce heat and boil gently, uncovered for 8 to 10 minutes or until currants have softened. Add cinnamon, allspice, cloves, and cream sherry; continue to cook for 5 to 6 minutes longer, stirring occasionally, until compote thickens.

Remove from heat, cool and refrigerate

Filling

4	8 oz. packages cream cheese, room temperature
1 1/4 c.	granulated sugar
1/4 tsp.	kosher salt
3 tbsp.	all-purpose flour

4	large eggs, room temperature
1 tsp.	pure vanilla extract
	Zest of 1 orange, finely minced
	Juice of 1 orange
3 tbsp.	cream sherry
1/4 c.	sour cream

In the large mixing bowl of a stand mixer fitted with the paddle attachment, beat the cream cheese, sugar, salt, and flour on medium-high speed, scraping down the bowl several times, until the mixture is smooth and fluffy for about 3 to 5 minutes. Turn the mixer to low and beat in the eggs one at a time, until blended, scraping down the sides of the bowl after each addition. Beat in vanilla, zest, orange juice, sherry, and sour cream until just blended, making sure not to overmix filling after the eggs are added.

Pour half of the filling over the crust in the prepared pan and spread out evenly. Carefully spoon half of the currant compote over filling into center of pan forming a 5 to 6 inch circle. Carefully pour remaining filling into pan spreading evenly.

Place the springform pan in a large enough roasting pan with 3-inch high sides and pour in enough boiling water to come halfway up the outside of the springform pan.

Bake for 1 hour and 10 minutes to 1 hour and 20 minutes or until edge is firm and center wobbles slightly when the pan is gently shaken.

Transfer cheesecake to a wire rack, remove foil, and cool for 1 hour. Using a small knife or metal spatula, cut around the rim to loosen crust from the side of the pan. Continue to cool to room temperature for about 4 hours. Chill the cheesecake, uncovered, in the pan for 8 hours or overnight before serving.

Cover the top of the cheesecake with the remaining currant compote and sprinkle top with the remaining 1/4 cup of almond slices. Keep refrigerated until just before serving. Enjoy!

Sweet Potato Cheesecake with Walnut Crust and Maple Buttercream Topping

Sweet Potato

2   sweet potatoes, 1 1/4 to 1 1/2 lbs

In a medium-size saucepan, over medium-high heat, boil the sweet potatoes until fork tender, about 30 to 35 minutes. Peel and cut sweet potatoes into chunks and mash in a bowl until smooth. Set aside to cool.

Chef's tip: Sweet potatoes can be prepared 2 to 3 days ahead of time, cover and refrigerate.

Crust

1 1/2 c.   graham cracker crumbs

1/2 c.   walnuts, finely chopped

1/4 c.   golden brown sugar, packed

1/4 tsp.   ground cinnamon

6 tbsp.   unsalted butter, melted

Preheat oven to 350°F.

Lightly butter a 9-inch springform pan with 2 3/4-inch high sides; wrap the outside of the pan with 2 layers of heavy-duty foil and set aside.

In a medium-size bowl combine the graham cracker crumbs, walnuts, brown sugar, and cinnamon until thoroughly mixed. Add the butter and with a fork, mix crumb mixture until evenly moistened and crumbs stick together when lightly pressed. Press crumb mixture over the bottom and 1 to 1 1/2 inches up the side of the cake pan. Set aside.

Filling

3	8 oz. packages cream cheese, room temperature
3/4 c.	granulated sugar
1/2 c.	golden brown sugar, packed
4	large eggs, room temperature
1 1/4 c.	reserved sweet potatoes
1/4 c.	heavy cream
1/4 c.	sour cream
1/4 c.	pure maple syrup
1 1/2 tsp.	ground cinnamon
1 tsp.	ground nutmeg
1/2 tsp.	ground ginger

In the bowl of a stand mixer fitted with the paddle attachment, beat the cream cheese on medium-high speed for 3 to 5 minutes or until smooth; scraping down the side of the bowl occasionally. Gradually add the granulated and brown sugar and continue to beat for 2 to 3 minutes until mixture is well blended and smooth. Turn the mixer to low speed and beat in the eggs one at a time until just blended; scraping down the side of the bowl after each addition. Add the sweet potato and mix until just blended. Add the cream, sour cream, maple syrup, cinnamon, nutmeg, and ginger and continue to mix until just blended making sure not to overmix after the eggs have been added.

Pour the filling over the crust in the prepared cake pan.

Place the springform pan into a large enough roasting pan, with 2- to 3-inch high sides, and pour enough boiling water into the roasting pan to come half way up the outside of the springform pan.

Bake for 1 hour and 20 minutes to 1 hour and 40 minutes or until the edge is firm and the center appears nearly set when the pan is gently shaken.

Remove the cheesecake from the oven to a wire rack, remove foil, and cool for 1 hour. Using a small knife or metal spatula, loosen the crust from the side of the pan by running it around the rim of the cake pan. Continue to cool to room temperature for about 4 hours. Refrigerate for 8 hours or overnight in the pan.

Maple Buttercream

1 c.	granulated sugar
3 tbsp.	water
	Pinch of kosher salt
1/4 c.	heavy cream
4 tbsp.	unsalted butter, cubed

2 oz.   cream cheese, cut into 1-inch cubes

1/4 c.   pure maple syrup

Bring to a boil the sugar, water, and salt in a medium saucepan over high-heat for 5 minutes, gently swirling occasionally to prevent scorching. Whisk in the cream and butter (mixture will bubble furiously; keep whisking). Boil 2 minutes longer.

Transfer the buttercream to the bowl of a stand mixer; whip on high-speed until side of the bowl is cool to the touch and mixture is thick, 8 to 10 minutes, scraping down side of the bowl as needed. Add cream cheese 1 cube at a time and beat until buttercream is smooth. Add maple syrup and mix until just blended.

Remove rim from the springform pan and transfer cheesecake to a serving dish. Spread buttercream over the top of the cheesecake and keep chilled until just before serving. Slice, serve and enjoy!

Mascarpone Cheesecake
with Biscotti Crust and Spicy Peach Sauce

Recipe inspired by Giada De Laurentiis

Crust

1 1/2 c.	purchased biscotti crumbs (2 packages)
1/4 c.	almonds, finely chopped, divided
1/4 c.	walnuts, finely chopped, divided
1/4 c.	granulated sugar
1/4 tsp.	anise extract
5 tbsp.	unsalted butter, melted

Preheat the oven to 350°F.

Butter a 9-inch springform pan with 2 3/4-inch high sides. Wrap the outside of the pan with 2 layers of heavy-duty foil.

In a food processor, finely grind biscotti.

Transfer crumbs to a medium-size bowl; add 1/8 cup almond, 1/8 cup walnuts, and sugar, mix to combine thoroughly. Add anise to the melted butter and stir to combine. Add butter and anise to crumb mixture and mix until crumbs are evenly moistened. Press mixture over the bottom of pan and 1 to 1 1/2 inches up side of the pan.

Bake crust for 12 to 15 minutes or until set and golden. Cool the crust on a wire rack completely and set aside.

Filling

2	8 oz. packages cream cheese, room temperature
2	8 oz. containers mascarpone cheese, room temperature
1 1/4 c.	granulated sugar
1/4 c.	peach brandy or peach liqueur
1 tsp.	pure vanilla extract
4	large eggs, room temperature

Decrease the oven temperature to 325°F.

Using a stand-up electric mixer fitted with a the paddle attachment, beat the cream cheese, mascarpone cheese, and sugar in a large bowl for 3 to 5 minutes or until fluffy and smooth , occasionally scraping down the side of the bowl. Beat in the brandy and vanilla until blended. Reduce mixer speed to low, add the eggs one at a time and beat until just blended, scraping down the side of the bowl after each addition. Pour the cheese mixture over the crust and spread evenly in the pan.

Place the springform pan in a large roasting pan with 2- to 3-inch sides, and pour enough boiling water into the roasting pan to come halfway up the outside of the springform pan.

Bake the cheesecake for 1 hour and 35 minutes or until the edge is firm and the center moves slightly when the pan is gently shaken.

Remove pan from the oven and transfer to a wire rack, remove foil and cool for 1 hour. Using a small knife or metal spatula, run it around the pan to loosen crust from the side of the pan. Refrigerate the cheesecake for 8 hours or overnight.

Peach Sauce

1 lb.	ripe peaches, peeled and chopped
1 c.	water
1/2	vanilla bean, split and seeded
2	whole cloves
1	cinnamon stick
3 tbsp.	granulated sugar

Place peaches in a large bowl, cover them with boiling water and leave for 20 to 30 seconds. Drain, peel, and chop the peaches.

Place the chopped peaches in a heavy-bottomed, medium-size saucepan with water, vanilla bean, cloves, and cinnamon stick. Bring to a boil, reduce the heat and simmer for 15 to 20 minutes or until the peaches are tender. Add the 3 tablespoons of sugar and stir over low heat until sugar dissolves. Increase the heat and simmer for 5 more minutes. Remove the vanilla bean and spices, cool slightly.

Pour sauce into a food processor and blend until smooth. Cover and refrigerate.

Cut cheesecake into wedges and spoon peach sauce over slices and serve. Enjoy!

Chef's tip: Sauce can be made 3 to 4 days ahead.

Vanilla Bean Cheesecake with Triple-Nut Filling and Vanilla Sauce

Crust

1 1/2 c.   graham cracker crumbs

1/4 c.   granulated sugar

1/4 c.   all-purpose flour

1/4 tsp.   kosher salt

6 tbsp.   unsalted butter, melted

Preheat oven to 350°F.

Lightly butter a 10-inch springform pan with 2 3/4-inch high sides. Wrap the outside of pan with 2 layers of heavy-duty foil.

In a medium-size bowl, thoroughly combine graham cracker crumbs, sugar, flour, and salt with a fork. Add melted butter to mixture and mix until crumbs are evenly moistened and stick together when lightly pressed. Press crumb mixture over bottom of prepared pan and 1 to 1 1/2 inches up side of the springform pan. Set aside.

Triple-nut filling

3/4 c.	dark brown sugar, packed
3	large eggs, room temperature
2/3 c.	dark corn syrup
6 tbsp.	unsalted butter, melted
1 tbsp.	molasses
1 1/2 tsp.	fresh lemon juice
1 tsp.	pure vanilla extract
1/4 tsp.	kosher salt
1/2 c.	black walnuts, coarsely broken
1/2 c.	slivered almonds
1/2 c.	pecan halves

In a large bowl beat brown sugar and eggs at medium speed until well-combined. Add corn syrup, butter, molasses, lemon juice, vanilla extract, and salt. Beat until combined.

Pour over crust in the prepared pan; sprinkle with black walnuts, slivered almonds, and pecans.

Bake 35 to 40 minutes or until filling is a light golden brown. (Filling will set as it cools.) Cool on a wire rack.

Reduce oven temperature to 325°F.

Chef's tip: Filling can be made 1 to 2 days ahead, lightly cover and refrigerate.

Filling

4	8 oz. packages cream cheese, room temperature
1 1/3 c.	granulated sugar
1/2 tsp.	kosher salt
2 tsp.	pure vanilla extract
1	vanilla bean, seeded
5	large eggs, room temperature
2/3 c.	sour cream

In the bowl of a stand mixer fitted with the paddle attachment, beat cream cheese, sugar, salt, vanilla extract, and vanilla seeds on medium-high speed for 3 to 5 minutes, scraping down sides of bowl several times, until mixture is creamy and smooth. Turn mixer to low speed, add eggs one at a time and beat until just blended, scraping down bowl after each addition. Beat in sour cream until just blended avoiding overmixing after eggs have been added. Gently pour filling over triple-nut filling and spread evenly.

Place the cake pan in a large roasting pan. Place both pans in the preheated oven and pour in enough boiling water to come about halfway up the outside of the springform pan.

Bake the cheesecake for 1 hour and 15 minutes to 1 hour and 20 minutes or until edge is set and center jiggles when the pan is gently shaken.

Remove springform pan from the oven to a wire rack, remove foil wrap, and cool for 1 hour. Using a small knife or metal spatula, cut around pan to loosen crust from the side of pan. Continue to cool cheesecake to room temperature for about 3 to 4 hours. Chill uncovered in the cake pan for 8 hours or overnight before serving.

Vanilla Sauce

10 oz.	heavy cream
1	vanilla bean, seeded
6 oz.	good-quality white chocolate, chopped (Lindt or Baker's)
1/4 c. ea.	black walnuts, slivered almonds, and pecans, coarsely chopped

Pour heavy cream into a small saucepan. Split vanilla bean and remove the seeds with a small knife; add seeds to the cream along with the pod. Over medium-high heat, bring cream vanilla mixture to a boil.

Remove saucepan from the heat, cover, and let stand for 10 minutes. Then, strain mixture through a fine-mesh strainer.

In a separate bowl, add chopped white chocolate. Reheat the cream and pour over chocolate and let stand for 2 minutes, stir until melted and mixture is smooth. Set aside and keep warm.

Remove side of springform pan form cheesecake and transfer to serving plate. Slice cheesecake and top with vanilla sauce; sprinkle with nuts and serve. Enjoy!

Chef's tip: Vanilla sauce can be made up to 1 week ahead. Tightly cover and refrigerate.

Irish Coffee Brownie Bottom Cheesecake with Graham Cracker Crust and Irish Coffee Sauce

Crust

1 1/4 c.	graham cracker crumbs
1/4 c.	light brown sugar, packed
1/4 tsp.	ground cinnamon
	Pinch kosher salt
8 tbsp.	unsalted butter, melted

Preheat oven to 350°F.

Lightly butter a 9-inch springform pan with 2 3/4-inch high sides; wrap outside of pan with 2 layers of heavy-duty foil.

In a medium-size bowl, add graham cracker crumbs, brown sugar, cinnamon, and salt; with a fork, mix until thoroughly combined. Mix in melted butter until crumb mixture is evenly moist and sticks together when lightly pressed. Transfer crust mixture to prepared pan; press over bottom and 1 to 1 1/2 inches up sides of pan.

Bake crust for 8 to 10 minutes or until set and golden brown. Cool on wire rack.

Irish Coffee Brownies

1 c.	milk chocolate morsels
1/2 c.	unsalted butter
1/2 c.	granulated sugar
2	large eggs, room temperature
1 tsp.	pure vanilla extract
2 tbsp.	Irish whiskey
2 tsp.	instant coffee
1 c.	all-purpose flour

In a small saucepan over low heat, combine milk chocolate morsels and butter; stir until chocolate is melted and mixture is smooth Remove saucepan from heat and cool to room temperature.

In a large mixing bowl, add sugar and eggs and beat until thick and lemon-colored. Gradually beat in chocolate mixture and vanilla extract. In a separate cup, combine Irish whiskey and instant coffee; stirring until dissolved. Add to chocolate mixture. Gradually blend in flour until just combined. Pour brownie mixture over crust in the prepared pan.

Bake for 25 minutes or until set. Transfer to wire rack and cool slightly while preparing filling. Reduce heat to 325°F.

Filling

3	8 oz. packages cream cheese, room temperature
3/4 c.	granulated sugar
1 tsp.	pure vanilla extract
3	large eggs, room temperature
1/2 c.	sour cream

In the bowl of a stand mixer fitted with the paddle attachment, beat cream cheese, sugar, and vanilla extract on medium-high speed until creamy and smooth for about 3 to 5 minutes. Add eggs one at a time, on low speed, mixing until just blended; scraping down side of bowl after each addition. Add sour cream and mix until just blended, making sure not to overmix after eggs have been added. Pour filling over brownie bottom—filling will almost come to top of pan.

Place springform pan in a large roasting pan with 2- to 3-inch high sides, and pour enough boiling water into roasting pan to come halfway up outside of the springform pan.

Bake for 55 to 60 minutes or until edge is set and center wobbles when pan is gently shaken.

Remove springform pan from oven and transfer to a wire rack, remove foil, and cool for 1 hour. Run a small knife or metal spatula around rim of pan to loosen crust from side of pan. Cool to room temperature for about 4 hours. Loosely cover and refrigerate for 8 hours or overnight.

Irish Coffee Sauce

10 oz.	heavy cream
1	vanilla bean, seeded
6 oz.	good quality white chocolate (Lindt or Baker's), chopped
3 tbsp.	Irish whiskey

2 1/2 tsp. instant coffee

Pour heavy cream into a small saucepan. Split vanilla bean and remove seeds with a small knife; add seeds to the cream along with the pod. Over medium-high heat, bring cream vanilla mixture to a boil. Remove saucepan from heat, cover, and let stand for 10 minutes; strain mixture through a fine-mesh strainer.

In a separate bowl add chopped white chocolate. Reheat cream and pour over chocolate and let stand for 2 minutes, then, stir until melted and mixture is smooth. In a separate cup, add Irish whiskey and instant coffee; stir until dissolved. Add to vanilla sauce and stir until well blended and sauce is smooth. Set aside and keep warm.

Remove side of springform pan from cheesecake and transfer to serving dish. Slice cheesecake and top with Irish coffee sauce and serve. Enjoy!

Chef's tip: Irish coffee sauce can be made up to 1 week ahead. Tightly cover and refrigerate.

Orange Cheesecake with Cashew Crust and Cranberry-Kumquat Compote

Crust

1 c.   cashews, very finely chopped

1 c.   graham cracker crumbs

1/2 c.   granulated sugar

8 tbsp.   unsalted butter, melted

Preheat oven to 350°F.

Lightly butter a 9-inch springform pan with 2 3/4-inch high sides. Wrap the outside of the pan with 2 layers of heavy-duty foil.

In a medium-size bowl, combine chopped cashews, graham crackers, and sugar and combine thoroughly. Add butter, and with a fork, mix until mixture is evenly moistened. Press crumb mixture over the bottom of pan and 1 to 1 1/2 inches up side of pan and set aside.

Filling

1 c.	fresh orange juice
1 c.	granulated sugar, divided
2 tbsp.	orange peel, finely grated
4	8 oz. packages cream cheese, room temperature
1 c.	sour cream
3 tbsp.	all-purpose flour
1/4 tsp.	kosher salt
5	large eggs, room temperature

Combine the orange juice, 1/4 cup sugar, and orange peel in a small saucepan over medium-high heat. Bring mixture to a boil, stirring until sugar dissolves. Reduce heat and simmer until mixture is reduced to 3/4 cup for about 10 minutes. Remove pan from heat and chill until cool.

Using a stand-up electric mixer fitted with a the paddle attachment, beat the cream cheese and the remaining 3/4 cup sugar in a large bowl until creamy and smooth for about 3 to 5 minutes. Mix in sour cream, flour, and salt until combined. On low speed, add eggs one at a time and beat until just blended, scraping down the side of bowl after each addition. Mix in cooled orange juice mixture until just blended. Pour filling into prepared pan over crust.

Place the springform pan in a large roasting pan. Pour enough boiling water into the roasting pan to come halfway up side of the springform pan.

Bake cheesecake for 1 hour and 35 minutes or until edge is set and center jiggles when the pan is gently shaken.

Remove cake from the roasting pan; remove foil and move pan to a wire rack and cool for 1 hour. Run a small knife or metal spatula around the rim to loosen crust from the side of the pan. Cool to room temperature for about 4 hours. Chill and refrigerate for 8 hours or overnight.

Compote

1	12 oz. bag fresh cranberries, thawed if frozen
1	8 oz. package kumquats, trimmed and quartered lengthwise
1/2 c.	water
3/4 c.	sugar
1 tbsp.	fresh ginger, finely chopped
1	whole star anise
1/8 tsp.	kosher salt

In a large heavy saucepan, combine together all of the ingredients and simmer, uncovered, stirring occasionally, until cranberries have popped for about 10 to 12 minutes. Remove star anise, and cool compote completely.

Chef's tip: Compote can be made up to 1 week ahead, cover and refrigerate.

Remove cheesecake from the refrigerator and remove pan sides, and place cake on a platter. Cover top of the cheesecake with the chilled compote in an even layer and serve. Enjoy!

Orange Liqueur Sauce (optional topping)

1 tsp.	orange rind, grated
1 1/2 c.	fresh orange juice
1/4 c.	granulated sugar
1/4 c.	Grand Marnier or Cointreau
2 tbsp.	cornstarch
6 tbsp.	water
2 tbsp.	unsalted butter

Place the orange rind, juice, sugar, and liqueur in a small saucepan over low heat. Mix the cornstarch and water in a small bowl and stir until smooth. Add the cornstarch mixture to saucepan and stir for 3 to 4 minutes or until sauce boils and thickens. Add butter and stir for another minute.

Cool to room temperature. Serve warm sauce over sliced cheesecake. Enjoy!

Chef's tip: Leftover compote and sauce can be served over vanilla ice cream or frozen yogurt.

Chocolate Bourbon-Pecan Cheesecake with Vanilla Wafer Crust and Vanilla-Pecan Sauce

Crust

1 1/4 c.   purchased vanilla wafers, finely ground

1/4 c.   granulated sugar

1/4 tsp.   kosher salt

5 tbsp.   unsalted butter, melted

Preheat oven to 350°F.

Lightly butter a 9-inch springform pan with 2 3/4-inch high sides; wrap the outside of the pan with 2 layers of heavy-duty foil.

In a medium-size bowl, combine vanilla wafer crumbs, sugar, and salt with a fork until thoroughly mixed. Add butter, and stir until mixture is evenly moistened and sticks together when lightly pressed. Press the crust mixture over the bottom and 1 to 1 1/2 inches up the side of the prepared pan. Set aside.

Pecan Filling

3/4 c.	dark brown sugar, packed
3	large eggs, room temperature
6 tbsp.	unsalted butter, melted
2/3 c.	dark corn syrup
2 tbsp.	bourbon
1 tbsp.	molasses
1 tsp.	pure vanilla extract
1/4 tsp.	kosher salt
1/3 c.	semi-sweet chocolate chips
1 1/2 c.	pecan halves

In a large bowl, beat the eggs and brown sugar on medium speed until well-blended. Beat in the melted butter, corn syrup, bourbon, molasses, vanilla, and salt until thoroughly blended. Sprinkle the chocolate chips over the top of the crust, top with pecan halves, and pour filling over the pecans.

Bake for 45 to 50 minutes or until a knife inserted in the center comes out moist but clean. Cool slightly on a wire rack.

Reduce oven temperature to 325°F.

Filling

3	8 oz. packages cream cheese, room temperature
3/4 c.	granulated sugar
3	large eggs, room temperature

1 tsp.   pure vanilla extract

1/2 c.   sour cream

In the bowl of a stand mixer fitted with the paddle attachment, beat the cream cheese and sugar on medium-high speed for 3 to 5 minutes or until smooth . With mixer on low speed, add eggs one at a time and beat until just blended, scraping down the side of the bowl after each addition. Add the vanilla and sour cream and mix until just blended making sure not to overmix. Pour the filling over cooked pecan filling.

Place the springform pan in a large roasting pan with 2- to 3-inch high sides, and pour in enough boiling water into the roasting pan to come halfway up the outside of the springform pan.

Bake for 50 to 55 minutes or until the edge is set and the center wobbles when the pan is gently shaken.

Transfer springform pan to a wire rack, remove foil, and cool for 1 hour. Run a small knife or metal spatula around the rim of the pan to loosen the crust from the side of the pan. Continue to cool to room temperature for about 4 hours. Refrigerate for 8 hours or overnight in the cake pan.

Vanilla Sauce

10 oz.   heavy cream

1   vanilla bean, seeded

6 oz.   good quality white chocolate (Lindt or Baker's), chopped

1/4 c.   toasted pecans, chopped

Pour cream into a small saucepan. Split the vanilla bean and remove the seeds with a small knife; add seeds to the cream along with the pod. Over medium-high heat, bring the cream mixture to a boil.

Remove saucepan from heat, cover, and let stand for 10 minutes. Strain the mixture through a fine-mesh strainer.

In a separate bowl, add the chopped white chocolate. Reheat the cream, pour over the chocolate and let stand for 2 minutes; then, stir until melted and the mixture is smooth. Stir in chopped roasted pecans, set aside, and keep warm.

Remove the rim of the springform pan from the cheesecake and transfer to a serving dish. Slice the cake and top slices with the vanilla sauce and serve. Enjoy!

Chef's tip: Vanilla pecan sauce can be made up to 1 week ahead. Tightly cover and refrigerate.

Christmas Eve and Christmas Day

Christmas is that special time of the year when loved ones gather together and bask in the magic of the season.

Whether the night before Christmas or Christmas day are intimate, calm-before-the-storm gatherings or big days of anticipation and celebration, elegant menus are sure to fill the bill for your holiday festivities.

Whether your extravagant menu accommodates your holiday style, dressed up to feel special and elegant, or dressed down for comfort and ease, dessert is the culmination of your loved ones dining experience.

After dinner has been enjoyed by all, it's time for that special dessert. Be bold, take a risk, and break from traditional desserts. Take your guests on a journey into the rich, lavish world of the cheesecake.

Christmas Cheesecake Suggestions

Arroz Con Dulce (Sweet Rice Pudding) Cheesecake
with Vanilla Wafer-Macadamia Nut Crust and Rum-Raisin Sauce 107

Indian Pudding Cheesecake
with Black Walnut Crust and Rice Brandy Sauce.. 57

A Journey Into The Rich Lavish World of Cheesecakes

Arroz Con Dulce (Sweet Rice Pudding) Cheesecake with Macadamia Nut Crust and Rum-Raisin Sauce

Arroz con dulce is a traditional Puerto Rican style rice pudding dessert served at Christmas time and special occasions.

Sweet Rice Pudding

1 c.	Arborio or other short grain rice
2 c.	water
3	whole cloves
1/2	cinnamon stick
6 oz.	evaporated milk
7 oz.	coconut cream (Coco López)
7 oz.	coconut milk
1/4 c.	coconut, shredded
1 tbsp.	pure vanilla extract

1/8 tsp.   ground nutmeg

1/2 tsp.   ground ginger

            Pinch kosher salt

1/4 c.   golden raisins, soaked in rum

In a heavy saucepan over medium heat, bring the rice and water to a boil. Lower the heat to simmer and add the cloves and cinnamon stick; stir gently. Let the rice cook (uncovered) for about 8 to 15 minutes until most of the water is absorbed and rice is fluffy .

Add the evaporated milk, coconut cream, coconut milk, shredded coconut, vanilla, nutmeg, ginger, and salt, and simmer (uncovered) over low heat until mixture thickens and becomes creamy, stirring frequently.

Remove saucepan from the heat and discard cloves and cinnamon stick. Drain the raisins and stir into the pudding.

Transfer rice pudding to container, cover tightly, and refrigerate until completely cooled. Rice pudding can be made 2 to 3 days in advance.

Chef's tip: For best results, soak rice in water for about two hours prior to cooking.

Warning: Don't eat the rice until it has completely cooled; hot, it can cause ill effects.

Crust

1 1/4 c.   purchased vanilla wafer cookies, finely ground

1/4 c.   macadamia nuts, finely chopped

1/4 c.   granulated sugar

1/4 tsp.   kosher salt

5 tbsp.   unsalted butter, melted

Preheat oven to 350°F.

Lightly butter a 10-inch springform pan with 2 3/4-inch high sides; wrap outside of pan with 2 layers of heavy-duty foil and set aside.

In a food processor, add the vanilla wafers and macadamia nuts; pulse until finely ground.

Transfer crumbs to a medium-size bowl, add sugar and salt and combine thoroughly with a fork. Add butter and mix until crumb mixture is evenly moistened and crumbs stick together when lightly pressed. Press crumb mixture over the bottom and 1 to 1 1/2 inches up the side of the prepared pan. Set aside.

Filling

4	8 oz. packages cream cheese, room temperature
1 1/3 c.	granulated sugar
1/2 tsp.	kosher salt
5	large eggs, room temperature
2 tsp.	pure vanilla extract
2/3 c.	sour cream
3 tbsp.	macadamia nut liqueur

In the bowl of a stand mixer fitted with the paddle attachment, beat the cream cheese for about 2 to 3 minutes until smooth. Add sugar and salt, and continue to beat until smooth and fluffy, scraping down the side of the bowl several times. Reduce mixer speed to low. Add eggs one at a time and beat until just blended, scraping down side of the bowl after each addition. Beat in vanilla, sour cream, and macadamia liqueur until just blended.

Spoon enough rice pudding over crust in the prepared pan to form a 3/4-inch layer of pudding. Carefully pour the filling over rice pudding—filling will come all the way to the top of the pan.

Place the springform pan in a large roasting pan with 2- to 3-inch high side, and pour in enough boiling water to come halfway up the side of the cake pan.

Bake for 1 hour and 10 minutes to 1 hour and 20 minutes or until edge is set and center wiggles when the pan is gently shaken.

Transfer cheesecake to a wire rack, remove foil, and cool for 1 hour. Using a small knife or metal spatula, cut around the rim to loosen the crust from the side of the pan. Continue to cool to room temperature for about 4 hours. Chill cheesecake for 8 hours or overnight in the pan.

Rum-Raisin Sauce

1 1/2 c.	dark rum
1/2 c.	golden raisins
1/2 c.	granulated sugar
1/4 c.	water
1/2 tsp.	ground cinnamon
1/4 tsp.	pure vanilla extract
1 tbsp.	fresh lemon zest, finely minced
1 tbsp.	fresh orange zest, finely minced
1/2 c.	coconut, shredded and toasted

In a medium-size bowl, add rum and raisins and soak about 1 hour or until raisins plumped.

In a heavy saucepan, over medium-high heat, bring sugar, water, and cinnamon to a boil and cook for 2 minutes. Add plumped raisins and rum to sauce pan and continue to cook for 5 minutes longer.

Remove saucepan from heat and add vanilla, lemon zest, and orange zest, cover and let sit for 5 to 10 minutes. Keep the cheesecake chilled until just before serving.

Remove cheesecake from the pan and transfer to a serving dish. Spoon sauce over slices of cheesecake and sprinkle with toasted coconut and serve. Enjoy!

Chef's tip: Sauce can be made 2 to 3 days ahead. Store in covered container and refrigerate.

To toast coconut, preheat oven to 350°F. Arrange the shredded coconut in a single layer on a large rimmed baking sheet. Toast the coconut in the oven for 10 to 12 minutes or until golden brown in color, stirring occasionally to toast evenly. Remove from the oven and let cool completely.

Scottish Dundee Cheesecake with Shortbread-English Walnut Crust and Scottish Orange Marmalade Topping

Crust

1 c.	purchased shortbread cookies, finely ground
1 c.	English walnuts, finely chopped
1/4 c.	granulated sugar
4 tbsp.	unsalted butter, melted

Preheat oven to 375°F.

Lightly butter a 10-inch springform pan with 2 3/4-inch high sides and wrap outside of the pan with 2 layers of heavy-duty foil.

In a food processor, finely grind the shortbread cookies and English walnuts.

Transfer crumbs to a medium-size bowl and add sugar; combine thoroughly with a fork. Add melted butter and mix until the crumbs are evenly moistened and stick together when lightly pressed. Press the crumb mixture over bottom and 1 to 1 1/2 inches up the side of the prepared pan.

Bake the crust for 10 to 12 minutes or until the edges are golden brown. Remove from the oven and set aside to cool on a wire rack. Reduce oven temperature to 325°F.

Filling

4	8 oz. packages cream cheese, room temperature
1 c.	demerara sugar
1/4 tsp.	kosher salt
1 tsp.	ground cinnamon
1 tsp.	mixed spice (recipe to follow)
3 tbsp.	all-purpose flour, plus 1/4 c. for dredging dried fruits
4	large eggs, room temperature
1/2 c.	sour cream
	Zest of 1 lemon, finely minced
1 tbsp.	black treacle (molasses)
4 tbsp.	brandy
1 c.	candied peel
1/2 c.	dried cherries
1 c.	dried currants
1 c.	sultanas (golden raisins)
1 c.	raisins
1 c.	blanched almonds

In the bowl of an electric stand mixer fitted with the paddle attachment, beat the cream cheese on medium-high speed for 3 to 5 minutes or until smooth. Add the sugar, salt, cinnamon, mixed spice and flour and mix for an additional 2 to 3 minutes. Reduce the mixer speed to low and beat in eggs one at a time, until just blended, scraping down side of the bowl after each addition. Beat in the sour cream, lemon zest, molasses, and brandy until evenly combined, making sure not to overmix after the eggs have been added.

In a large sealable plastic storage bag, add candied peel, cherries, currants, sultanas, raisins, and 3 to 4 tablespoons of all-purpose flour. Seal the bag and shake vigorously until fruit is coated with the flour. Remove flour-coated fruit from the bag and shake off any excess flour.

Pour half the filling into the prepared cake pan and sprinkle half of the fruit mixture onto the filling. With a small metal spatula swirl the fruit into the filling. Repeat procedure with the remaining filling and fruit. Starting in the center of the cheesecake, gently place the blanched almonds in a circular pattern to cover the top of the cheesecake.

Place the springform pan in a large roasting pan with 2- to 3-inch high sides, and pour in enough boiling water into the roasting pan to come half way up the outside of the springform pan.

Bake for 1 hour to 1 hour and 10 minutes or until the edge is set and the center wobbles when the pan is gently shaken.

Remove the springform pan from the water bath and transfer to a wire rack, remove foil wrap, and cool for 1 hour. Run a small knife or metal spatula around rim of the pan to loosen the crust from the side of the pan. Cool to room temperature for about 4 hours. Chill for 8 hours or overnight in pan.

Mixed Spice

1 tsp.   ground cinnamon

1 tsp.   ground coriander

1 tsp.   ground nutmeg

1/2 tsp.   ground ginger

1/4 tsp.   ground allspice

1/4 tsp.   ground cloves

In a small bowl combine the cinnamon, coriander, nutmeg, ginger, allspice, and cloves, and mix thoroughly.

Makes about 2 tablespoons

Orange Marmalade Topping

1   16 oz. purchased jar of orange marmalade (Keiller Dundee Orange Marmalade or Duerr's 1881 Original)

For topping: In a small saucepan over medium heat, warm the marmalade until almost liquid. Spread the marmalade over the entire top of the cheesecake and chill until just before serving. Slice, serve and enjoy!

Traditional Hard Sauce (optional topping)

12 tbsp.   unsalted butter, softened

1 1/4 c.   confectioners' sugar

1   Pinch kosher salt

1 tsp.   pure vanilla extract

3–4 tbsp. brandy, or to taste

In a medium bowl beat the butter with an electric mixer on high speed until the butter is fluffy. Reduce mixer speed to low and gradually add the confectioners' sugar. When the sugar is well blended, set mixer speed back to high. Add the salt and vanilla extract and beat until just blended. Add the brandy 1 tablespoon at a time and beat until combined and to desired taste. Spread the hard sauce on top of the cheesecake and serve. Enjoy!

Chef's tip: Hard sauce can be made up to a week ahead, cover tightly and refrigerate. Allow hard sauce to come to room temperature for 20 to 30 minutes before serving.

Blackcurrant Cheesecake
with Graham Cracker-English Walnut Crust and Blackcurrant Glaze

Crust

1 1/2 c.	graham cracker crumbs
1/2 c.	English walnuts, toasted, finely chopped
1/4 c.	granulated sugar
1/2 tsp.	ground cinnamon
6 tbsp.	unsalted butter, melted

Preheat the oven to 350°F.

Lightly butter a 9-inch springform pan with 2 3/4-inch high sides and wrap outside of the pan with 2 layers of heavy-duty foil.

In a medium-size bowl, combine graham cracker crumbs, toasted nuts, sugar, and cinnamon. Add melted butter and blend with a fork until mixture is evenly moistened and crumbs stick together when lightly pressed. Press mixture over the bottom of the prepared pan and 1 to 1 1/2 inches up the side of the pan.

Bake crust until set and lightly browned, about 8 to 10 minutes. Remove from oven and cool on a wire rack. Set aside.

Blackcurrants

1 1/4 c.	blackcurrants, fresh
4 tbsp.	granulated sugar
2 tbsp.	lemon juice
1/4 c.	water or Crème de Cassis
1 tbsp.	cornstarch

In a medium-size saucepan, add the blackcurrants, sugar, and lemon juice; heat the mixture over low heat until it begins to simmer. In a separate small bowl, whisk the cornstarch with 2 tablespoons of water into smooth slurry and add to saucepan. Continue to simmer until mixture thickens and the currants become soft.

Remove pan from the heat and pour off a 1/4 cup of the liquid into a bowl; add 1/4 cup of the cooked currants to the liquid and puree until smooth. Set aside. Take an additional 1/4 cup of cooked currants and set aside for the glaze.

Allow the remaining currants to cool. Then spread the cooled mixture over the prepared crust

Filling

4	8 oz. packages cream cheese, room temperature
1 1/4 c.	granulated sugar
4	large eggs, room temperature

2 tbsp.	all-purpose flour
2 tbsp.	fresh lemon juice
2 tsp.	freshly grated lemon zest
2 tsp.	pure vanilla extract
1/2 c.	sour cream

In the bowl of a stand mixer fitted with the paddle attachment, beat the cream cheese and sugar on medium-high speed for 3 to 5 minutes, scraping down side of the bowl several times, until mixture is smooth and fluffy. Turn the mixer to low, and beat in the eggs one at a time, until just blended and scraping down the side of the bowl after each addition. Add flour, lemon juice, zest, vanilla extract, and sour cream and combine until just blended, making sure not to overmix after eggs have been added.

Pour filling over currants and crust in the prepared pan, and tap gently on the countertop several times to remove any air bubbles from the filling.

Place the springform pan in a large roasting pan with 2- to 3-inch high sides, and pour in enough boiling water into the roasting pan to come halfway up the outside of the springform pan.

Bake for 1 hour to 1 hour and 15 minutes or until outer edge is set and center jiggles when the pan is gently shaken.

Remove springform pan to a wire rack, remove foil, and cool for 1 hour. Using a small knife or metal spatula, loosen the crust from the side of the pan by running it around the cake. Continue to cool cheesecake to room temperature for about 3 to 4 hours. Cover and refrigerate for 8 hours or overnight in pan.

Glaze

1/2 c.   granulated sugar

1 tsp.   cornstarch

1/4 tsp.   kosher salt

3/4 c.   water

1/2 c.   ea. reserved currant purée and cooked currants

1   egg yolk, well beaten

1 tbsp.   unsalted butter

In a medium-size sauce pan, combine sugar, cornstarch, salt, and water.

In a separate bowl, whisk together the reserved blackcurrant purée and well-beaten egg yolk; add to the saucepan and cook over low heat until the mixture is thick and smooth. Whisk in butter and continue to cook until butter has melted and is well blended in. Remove pan from heat and gently stir in reserved 1/4 cup of currants and set aside to cool.

Remove side of pan from the chilled cheesecake and transfer to a serving plate. When the glaze has cooled enough, but not so thick that it cannot be spread, spoon the glaze onto the cake and spread evenly over the top of the cheesecake. Chill until just before serving. Serve and enjoy!

Eggnog Cheesecake with Cashew Crust and Brandy Buttercream Topping

Crust

1 c.	cashews, finely chopped
1 c.	graham cracker crumbs
1/2 c.	granulated sugar
8 tbsp.	unsalted butter, melted

Preheat oven to 350°F.

Lightly butter a 10-inch springform pan with 2 3/4-inch high sides and wrap outside of the pan with 2 layers of heavy-duty foil.

In a medium-size bowl, combine cashews, graham cracker crumbs, and sugar. Add butter and with a fork, mix until evenly moistened and crumbs stick together when lightly pressed. Press the mixture evenly over the bottom and 1 to 1 1/2 inches up the side of the pan; set aside.

Filling

4	8 oz. packages cream cheese, room temperature
1 c.	granulated sugar
1 tsp.	pure vanilla extract
1/2 tsp.	ground nutmeg
1 tbsp.	brandy (optional)
3	large eggs, room temperature
1 1/2 c.	purchased eggnog

In the bowl of a stand mixer fitted with the paddle attachment, beat the cream cheese and sugar on medium-high speed for 3 to 5 minutes or until smooth, scraping down the side of the bowl occasionally. Beat in vanilla, nutmeg, and brandy for an additional 2 to 3 minutes or until well-blended. Turn the mixer to low and beat in the eggs one at a time, until just blended making sure not to overmix after the eggs have been added.

Pour filling over the crust into the prepared pan.

Place the springform pan in a large roasting pan with 2- to 3-inch high sides, and pour in enough boiling water into the roasting pan to come halfway up the outside of the springform pan.

Bake cheesecake for 1 hour and 15 minutes to 1 hour and 30 minutes or until edge is firm and center jiggles when the pan is gently shaken.

Remove cake pan to a wire rack, remove foil, and cool for 1 hour. Run a small knife or metal spatula around rim of the pan to loosen the crust from the side of the pan. Continue to cool cheesecake to room temperature for about 4 hours. Refrigerate 8 hours or overnight in pan.

Buttercream Topping

1 c.   granulated sugar

3 tbsp.   water

            Pinch of kosher salt

1/4 c.   heavy cream

4 tbsp.   unsalted butter, cubed

2 oz.   cream cheese, cut into 1-inch cubes

1 tbsp.   brandy

1/4 c.   cashews, coarsely chopped

Boil sugar, water and salt in a large saucepan over high heat for 5 minutes, gently swirling occasionally to prevent scorching. Whisk in cream and butter pieces (mixture will bubble furiously; keep whisking). Boil 2 minutes more.

Transfer mixture to the bowl of a stand mixer, and whip on high speed for 8 to 10 minutes or until side of the bowl is cool to the touch and buttercream is thick; scraping down the side of the bowl as needed. Add cream cheese, one cube at a time, until buttercream is smooth. Add brandy and mix until just blended.

Remove rim from springform pan and transfer cheesecake to a serving platter. Evenly spread buttercream over top of the cheesecake and sprinkle with chopped cashews. Keep chilled until just before serving. Enjoy!

Mascarpone Cheesecake with Toasted Pecan-Walnut Crust and Quince Compote Topping

Crust

1/2 c.   pecans, toasted, finely chopped

1/2 c.   walnuts, toasted, finely chopped

1 c.   graham cracker crumbs

1/4 c.   golden brown sugar

6 tbsp.   unsalted butter, melted

Preheat the oven to 375°F.

Lightly butter a 9-inch springform pan with 2 3/4-inch high sides and wrap the outside of pan with 2 layers of heavy-duty foil.

In a food processor, finely chop toasted pecans and walnuts.

Transfer chopped nuts to a medium-size bowl, add graham cracker crumbs, and brown sugar and combine thoroughly with a fork. Add melted butter to crumb mixture and combine until evenly moistened and crumbs stick together when lightly pressed. Press mixture over bottom of the prepared pan and 1 to 1 1/2 inches up the side.

Bake crust for 10 to 12 minutes or until set and golden brown. Cool on a wire rack completely and set aside.

Filling

2	8 oz. packages cream cheese, room temperature
2	8 oz. containers mascarpone cheese, room temperature
1 1/4 c.	granulated sugar
	Pinch kosher salt
2 tbsp.	all-purpose flour
1	vanilla bean, seeded
4	large eggs, room temperature
1/2 c.	sour cream

Reduce oven temperature to 325°F

In the bowl of a stand mixer fitted with the paddle attachment, beat the cream cheese, mascarpone, sugar, and salt for about 3 to 5 minutes or until smooth and fluffy occasionally scraping down the side of the bowl. Beat in vanilla seeds for 1 to 2 minutes more or until blended. Add the eggs one at a time on low speed and mix until just blended, scraping down the bowl after each addition. Add sour cream and mix until just combined making sure not to overmix after the eggs have been added.

Pour filling into prepared pan and tap gently on the countertop several times to remove air bubbles from filling.

Place the springform pan in a large roasting pan with 2- to 3-inch high sides, and pour enough boiling water into the roasting pan to come halfway up the outside of the springform pan.

Bake the cheesecake for 1 hour 40 minutes or until the edge is set and center wiggles when the pan is gently shaken.

Remove springform pan from the oven and transfer to a wire rack, remove foil, and cool for 1 hour. Using a small knife or metal spatula, cut around edge of pan to loosen crust from the side of the cake pan. Cool to room temperature for about 4 hours, loosely cover, and refrigerate for 8 hours or overnight and up to 2 days.

Quince Compote

4	quinces, peeled and quartered
2 c.	water
2 c.	granulated sugar
2 c.	white wine (Vouvray, Chenin-Blanc)
1	3-inch strip lemon zest
1	cinnamon stick
1	star anise pod
1	vanilla bean, seeded

In a large heavy saucepan, over medium-high heat, bring to a boil quinces, water, sugar, wine, lemon zest, cinnamon stick, and star anise pod, stirring mixture often. Reduce heat to low and add seeds of vanilla bean and vanilla bean pod to sauce pan. Cover and simmer for 15 to 25 minutes or until fruit is soft and is easily pierced with a knife, stirring occasionally .

Using a slotted spoon, transfer cooked fruit to a bowl.

Strain remaining juice through a fine-mesh strainer into another saucepan. Increase heat to medium-high and boil liquid for 40 to 50 minutes or until reduced by approximately one half. Pour syrup over the fruit, cover and chill overnight.

When ready to serve, warm compote and spoon over sliced cheesecake. Enjoy!

Chef's tip: Quince compote can be made up to 1 week ahead, keep tightly covered and refrigerated.

How to freeze quinces:

Because the availability of quinces has such a short season here in the Northeast (mid-November to mid-December), I am including a simple way of preserving this rock-hard fruit by freezing them.

Wash the quinces, remove any brown spots, and rub away the down from the skin.

Place the quinces in a large pan and barely cover them with cold water. Regulate the heat so that the water slowly comes to a boil and the fruit barely simmers. Depending on the heat, do this for 1 to 2 hours or until they start showing signs of softening. Stop when the skins start splitting or else they will quickly disintegrate. Watch the quinces while they very, very gently simmer away and remove them from the heat when softened but still whole. Leave them to cool in the pan until the next day.

When cool lift the quinces from the cooking water [if you are short on time, pop them in the freezer as they are], quarter them and remove the cores, this is done almost effortlessly compared with the raw fruit.

Open freeze all the quartered pieces on a tray. Then bag them in freezer bags the next day.

Courtesy of Maria Fremlin, October 22, 2010

Clementine-Date Cheesecake with Spicy Date Filling and Poached Clementines in a Grand Marnier Sauce

Spicy Date Filling

1 1/2 c.	dried pitted dates, chopped
1/4 c.	light brown sugar
1 tsp.	orange zest
1/4 tsp.	ground cloves
1/2 tsp.	ground cinnamon
1/4 tsp.	ground allspice
1 1/2 tsp.	fresh lemon juice
7/8 c.	water

Combine all of the ingredients in a small saucepan and cook over medium-high heat, stirring constantly until the dates are soft and the mixture becomes a thick paste, about 10 minutes. Remove the saucepan from heat and set aside to cool.

Chef's note: spicy date filling can be made 1 to 2 days ahead. Cover tightly and refrigerate.

Crust

1 c.   purchased vanilla wafer cookies, finely ground

1 c.   toasted walnuts, finely chopped

1/4 c.   light brown sugar, packed

4 tbsp.   unsalted butter, melted

Preheat oven to 325°F.

Lightly butter a 9-inch diameter springform pan with 2 3/4-inch high sides. Wrap the outside of cake pan with 2 layers of heavy-duty foil.

In a food processor, add vanilla wafers and toasted walnuts; pulse until mixture is finely ground.

Transfer crumbs to a medium-sized bowl, add brown sugar and combine thoroughly with a fork. Add butter and blend until evenly moistened and crumbs stick together when lightly pressed. Press crust mixture over the bottom and 1 to 1 1/2 inches up the side of the prepared pan. Spoon date filling into prepared pan spreading evenly over the bottom the crust. Set aside

Filling

2   8 oz. packages cream cheese, room temperature

2   8 oz. containers mascarpone cheese, room temperature

1 1/4 c.   granulated sugar

1   vanilla bean, seeds only

1 tsp.   pure vanilla extract

4   large eggs, room temperature

Using a stand-up mixer fitted with the paddle attachment, beat the cream cheese, mascarpone cheese, and sugar until smooth, about 3 to 5 minutes, occasionally scraping down the side of the bowl. Beat in vanilla seeds and vanilla extract until just blended. Reduce the mixer speed to low; add eggs one at a time and beat until blended, scraping down side of the bowl after each addition, making sure not to overmix after eggs have been added.

Pour filling over date filling and crust and gently tap springform pan on the countertop several times to remove air bubbles from the filling.

Place the springform pan in a large roasting pan and pour enough boiling water into the roasting pan to come halfway up the outside of the springform pan.

Bake the cheesecake for 1 hour and 30 minutes or until edge is firm and center moves slightly when the pan is gently shaken.

Remove springform from the oven and transfer to a wire rack, remove foil, and cool for 1 hour. Using a small knife or metal spatula, cut around edge of pan to loosen crust from side of pan. Cool cake to room temperature for about 4 hours. Cover and refrigerate for 8 hours or overnight and up to 2 days in pan.

Poached Clementines

7	clementines, peeled, pith removed, and segmented
2 c.	water
1 c.	granulated sugar
1 c.	Grand Marnier

In a saucepan, add water and sugar and bring to a boil over medium-high heat. Reduce heat to low and simmer for 10 to 15 minutes or until liquid has reduced by almost half forming a light syrup . Add Grand Marnier and clementine segments to syrup.

Remove saucepan from heat, and let clementines cool in poaching liquid. Reserve the poaching liquid for Grand Marnier sauce.

Grand Marnier Sauce

1 c.	reserved poaching liquid
2 c.	clementine juice, or orange juice
1 tsp.	clementine peel, grated
1 1/2 tbsp. cornstarch	
1/4 c.	water
1/2 c.	crème fraîche

In a small saucepan, combine poaching liquid, juice, and clementine peel; cook mixture over medium heat until liquid is reduced by half. Mix the cornstarch with 1/4 cup water, rapidly whisk cornstarch mixture into boiling syrup.

Cook for 3 minutes until thickened; remove saucepan from heat and cool. Stir in crème fraîche and refrigerate.

Remove side of springform pan from cheesecake and transfer to a serving dish. Top slices of cheesecake with poached clementine segments and Grand Marnier sauce. Serve and enjoy!

Greek Cheesecake with Baked Fig Filling and Poached Fig Topping

Baked Figs

8	fresh Calimyrna figs (when available) or dried
1/4 c.	wildflower honey, slightly warmed
1/4 c.	Ouzo
1	lemon, zested and juiced
2	bay leaves
1/4 c.	slivered almonds, toasted

Preheat oven to 350°F.

Place the figs in a medium-size, non-metallic baking dish. In a small bowl, combine honey, Ouzo, and lemon juice and pour mixture over the figs. Sprinkle the figs with lemon zest and tuck the bay leaves amongst the figs.

Cover the baking dish with foil and bake for 20 minutes or until the figs are tender and soft.

Remove baking dish from oven and transfer to a wire rack; cool to room temperature.

Crust

1 1/2 c.   purchased shortbread cookies, finely ground

1/2 c.   almonds, finely chopped

1/4 c.   granulated sugar

1/4 tsp.   anise extract

6 tbsp.   unsalted butter, melted

Increase oven temperature to 400°F.

Lightly butter a 9-inch springform pan with 2 3/4-inch high sides. Wrap the outside of the pan with 2 layers of heavy-duty foil and set aside.

In a food processor, grind shortbread cookies and almonds until finely chopped.

Transfer crumbs to a medium-size bowl, add sugar and combine thoroughly with a fork. Stir anise into melted butter and pour over crumb mixture; blend until evenly moistened and crumbs stick together when lightly pressed. Press crust mixture over the bottom and 1 to 1 1/2 inches up the side of the prepared pan.

Bake crust for 6 to 8 minutes or until lightly browned. Remove from the oven and cool on a wire rack. Reduce oven temperature to 350°F.

Cover the bottom of the crust with a single layer of cooled baked figs; sprinkle with toasted slivered almonds and set aside.

Filling

4   8 oz. packages cream cheese, room temperature

1 1/4 c.   granulated sugar

4   large eggs, room temperature

3/4 c.	plain Greek yogurt

1 tbsp.	pure vanilla extract

In the bowl of a stand mixer, fitted with the paddle attachment, beat together the cream cheese and sugar on medium-high speed for 3 to 5 minutes or until creamy and smooth . Reduce mixer speed to low. Add the eggs one at a time beating until just blended; scraping down the side of the bowl after each addition. Add the yogurt and vanilla and beat until just blended, making sure not to overmix after the eggs have been added.

Pour filling over figs and crust in the prepared pan. Tap the cake pan on the countertop several times to release any trapped air bubbles.

Place the springform pan into a large roasting pan with 2- to 3-inch high sides and pour enough boiling water into the roasting pan to come halfway up the outside of the springform pan.

Bake for 1 hour and 10 minutes or until the edge is set and the center wobbles when the pan is gently shaken.

Remove cheesecake from the oven and transfer to a wire rack, remove foil, and cool for 1 hour. Using a small knife or metal spatula, cut around the rim of the pan to loosen crust from side of the springform pan. Cool to room temperature, about 4 hours. Refrigerate cheesecake for 8 hours or overnight in the pan.

Fig Topping

16	whole Calimyrna figs, dried
2 c.	warm water
1/2 c.	Ouzo
1	cinnamon stick
1	3-inch strip orange zest

1/2 c.   granulated sugar

Place the figs in a small bowl, cover with warm water and let soak for 1 hour. Strain the figs and reserve the soaking water.

Strain the soaking liquid into a medium-size saucepan, add Ouzo and bring to a boil over high heat. To the saucepan, add the cinnamon stick, orange zest, and the figs. Reduce the heat to medium, and cook for 10 to 15 minutes or until the figs are plump and the liquid is the consistency of thin syrup.

With a slotted spoon, remove figs from the saucepan and set aside to cool. Add sugar to the saucepan and stir until sugar is dissolved, reduce heat to maintain a gentle simmer. Cook until the syrup is reduced by half, or for about 15 to 25 minutes.

Remove the cinnamon stick and orange zest and discard. Chop the cooled figs and return them to the syrup. Slice the cheesecake and serve with fig topping. Enjoy!

Chef's tip: Baked figs and fig topping can be made up to 1 week ahead of time. When honey is slightly warmed, it will pour easier than if at room temperature.

Inspiration source:

Recipes from A Greek Island by Susie Jacobs Coran. Octopus Limited, 1993

Chocolate Truffle Cheesecake
with Chocolate Wafer Crust and Hazelnut Topping

Crust

1 1/2 c.   purchased chocolate wafer cookies, finely ground

1/4 c.   English walnuts, toasted and finely ground

1 tbsp.   all-purpose flour

6 tbsp.   unsalted butter, melted

Preheat oven to 350°F.

Lightly butter a 9-inch springform pan with 2 3/4-inch high sides and wrap the outside of the cake pan with 2 layers of heavy-duty foil.

In a medium-size bowl, combine the chocolate wafer crumbs, walnuts, and flour and mix thoroughly with a fork. Stir in the melted butter, and blend until mixture is evenly moistened and the crumbs stick together when lightly pressed. Press the crumb mixture onto bottom and 1 to 1 1/2 inches up the side of the cake pan and set aside.

Filling

8	1 oz. squares semisweet chocolate, melted and slightly cooled
1/4 c.	water
4	8 oz. packages cream cheese, room temperature
1 c.	granulated sugar
1/4 tsp.	kosher salt
1 tsp.	pure vanilla extract
2 tbsp.	all-purpose flour
4	large eggs, room temperature
1/4 c.	hazelnut liqueur
1/4 c.	sour cream

In a double boiler or bain-marie over gently simmering water, add the chopped chocolate and 1/4 cup water, and stir until chocolate is melted and smooth. Remove pan from the heat and cool slightly.

In the bowl of a stand mixer fitted with the paddle attachment, beat the cream cheese on medium-high speed for 3 to 5 minutes or until smooth. Add the sugar, salt, vanilla, and flour and mix for an additional 2 to 3 minutes. Reduce mixer speed to low. Beat in the eggs one at a time until just blended, scraping down side of the bowl after each addition. Beat in the melted chocolate, hazelnut liqueur, and sour cream until evenly blended, making sure not to overmix after the eggs have been added.

Pour filling over the crust in the prepared pan, and tap pan several times on the countertop to release any air bubbles in the filling.

Place the springform pan in a large roasting pan with 2- to 3-inch high sides, and pour in enough boiling water to come halfway up the outside of the springform pan.

Bake the cheesecake for 1 hour to 1 hour and 15 minutes or until edges appear set and center wiggles when the pan is gently shaken.

Remove the springform pan from the oven and transfer to a wire rack, remove foil, cool for 1 hour. Using a small knife or metal spatula, cut around the rim of the pan to loosen crust from the side of the springform pan. Continue to cool the cheesecake to room temperature, about 4 hours. Refrigerate cheesecake for 8 hours or overnight in the pan.

Topping

1/2 c.   apricot jam

1/2 c.   hazelnuts, toasted and coarsely chopped

1/2 c.   English walnuts, toasted and coarsely chopped

1 tbsp.   unsweetened cocoa powder

In a small saucepan, warm the jam over low heat until liquid. Strain the jam through a fine strainer.

In a separate bowl, combine the hazelnuts and walnuts together. Brush the top of the cheesecake with jam and sprinkle nuts on top of the cake until entire top is covered. Using a fine strainer, dust the top of the nuts with cocoa powder. Refrigerate until just before serving. Serve and enjoy!

Bourbon Cheesecake
with Pecan-Date Crust and Bourbon-Molasses
Buttercream Topping

Crust

1/2 c.	toasted pecans, finely chopped
12	dates, pitted and chopped
3/4 c.	graham cracker crumbs
1/4 c.	light brown sugar, packed
5 tbsp.	unsalted butter, melted

Preheat oven to 350°F.

Lightly butter a 9-inch springform pan with 2 3/4-inch sides, and wrap the pan with 2 layers of heavy duty foil.

In a food processor, pulse toasted pecans and dates until finely ground.

Transfer nut-date mixture to a medium-size bowl, add graham cracker crumbs and brown sugar; mix thoroughly with a fork. Add the melted butter and combine until crust mixture is evenly moistened and crumbs stick together when lightly pressed. Press mixture over the bottom and 1 to 1 1/2 inches up the side of the pan. Set aside.

Filling

4	8 oz. packages cream cheese, room temperature
3/4 c.	light brown sugar, packed
1/4 tsp.	kosher salt
2 tbsp.	all-purpose flour
6	large eggs, room temperature
1/4 c.	heavy cream
1/4 c.	bourbon

Using a stand mixer fitted with the paddle attachment beat the cream cheese on medium-high speed for 3 to 5 minutes or until fluffy and free of lumps. Add the brown sugar, salt, and flour, and continue to beat mixture for 2 to 3 minutes more or until well combined, scraping the sides of the bowl occasionally. Turn mixer speed to low and add eggs one at a time, beating until just blended, scraping down the bowl after each addition. Add heavy cream and bourbon and mix until just blended making sure not to overmix after the eggs have been added.

Pour filling over crust in the prepared pan.

Place the springform pan in a large roasting pan and pour in enough boiling water to come halfway up the outside of the springform pan.

Bake for 1 hour to 1 hour and 10 minutes or until edge is set and the center wobbles when the pan is gently shaken.

Remove springform pan from the oven and transfer to a wire rack, remove foil, and cool for 1 hour. Using a small knife or metal spatula, cut around pan to loosen crust from the side of the cake pan. Continue to cool the cheesecake to room temperature for about 4 hours. Chill for 8 hours or overnight in the pan.

Bourbon-Molasses Buttercream

1 c.	granulated sugar
3 tbsp.	water
	Pinch of kosher salt
1/4 c.	heavy cream
4 tbsp.	unsalted butter, cubed
2 oz.	cream cheese, cut into 1/2-inch cubes
2 tbsp.	molasses
2 tbsp.	bourbon
1/4 c.	toasted pecan halves

In a medium saucepan over high heat, bring to a boil the sugar, water, and salt, and boil for about 5 minutes; gently swirling occasionally to prevent scorching. Whisk in cream and butter pieces (mixture will bubble furiously; keep whisking). Boil for 2 minutes more.

Transfer sugar syrup to the bowl of a stand mixer; whip on high speed for 8 to 10 minutes or until side of the bowl is cool to the touch and syrup is thick, scraping down sides of bowl as needed. Add cream cheese one cube at a time until buttercream is smooth. Stir in molasses and bourbon mixing until thoroughly blended.

Remove side of pan from the chilled cheesecake and transfer to a serving plate. Spread buttercream over the top of cheesecake covering evenly and sprinkle with toasted pecan halves. Keep chilled until just before serving. Enjoy!

Chef's tip: Buttercream can be made up to 1 week ahead. Cover tightly and refrigerate.

Bruce A. Williamson

Rum Raisin Cheesecake with Rum-Pecan Caramel Sauce

Crust

3/4 c.   purchased shortbread cookies, finely ground 3/4 c. pecans, finely chopped

1/4 c.   granulated sugar

4 tbsp.   unsalted butter, melted

Preheat oven to 350°F.

Lightly butter a 9-inch springform pan with 2 3/4-inch high sides. Wrap outside of pan with 2 layers of heavy-duty foil.

In a medium-size bowl, combine shortbread crumbs, sugar, and pecans. Add melted butter and blend with a fork until crust mixture is evenly moistened. Press the mixture into the bottom and 1 to 1 1/2 inches up the side of prepared pan.

Bake crust for 12 minutes or until set and a deep golden brown. Remove from oven and set aside to cool on a wire rack.

Filling

5	8 oz. packages cream cheese, room temperature
1 1/2 c.	granulated sugar
1 tbsp.	vanilla extract
6	large eggs, room temperature
4	large egg yolks, room temperature
1/2 c.	dark rum
1/3 c.	half-and-half
1 c.	golden raisins

In the bowl of a stand mixer fitted with the paddle attachment, beat the cream cheese, sugar, and vanilla extract on medium-high speed for 5 to 8 minutes , scraping down bowl several times, or until the mixture is smooth and fluffy. Turn the mixer to low and beat in the eggs one at a time until just blended, scraping down the sides of the bowl after each addition. Beat in egg yolks the same as the eggs, one at a time. Stir in the rum, raisins, and half-and-half until just blended. Do not overmix filling after eggs have been added.

Pour filling over crust in prepared pan.

Place springform pan into a roasting pan with 3-inch high sides. Pour in enough boiling water to come halfway up the outside of the springform pan.

Bake for 1 hour and 30 minutes or until the edge is firm and the center wobbles when gently shaken.

Transfer cake pan to a wire rack and cool for 1 hour. Using a small knife or metal spatula, cut around the rim to loosen crust from the side of the pan. Cool to room temperature for about 4 hours. Chill for 8 hours or overnight in the refrigerator.

Rum-Pecan Caramel Sauce

1/2 c.	granulated sugar
3 tbsp.	dark spiced rum plus 2 tsp.
3 tbsp.	water
1 tsp.	fresh lemon juice
1/4 c.	heavy cream
1 tsp.	pure vanilla extract
1/4 c.	pecans, coarsely chopped
1/2 c.	sweetened flaked coconut, toasted

Combine sugar, 3 tablespoons rum, water, and lemon juice in a medium saucepan over medium-high heat; cook for 2 minutes or until sugar dissolves, stirring constantly. Bring mixture to a boil; reduce heat to medium and cook, without stirring 10 minutes longer or until golden in color.

Remove saucepan from heat. Carefully add cream, stirring constantly (mixture will bubble vigorously). Cool caramel slightly. Stir in remaining 2 teaspoons rum, vanilla, and chopped pecans. Caramel sauce can be made up to three days ahead, cover and refrigerate.

To serve, warm sauce and spoon onto slices of cheesecake and sprinkle with toasted coconut. Serve and enjoy!

Chef's tip: To toast coconut, place coconut on a rimmed baking sheet in a 350°F oven for 10 to 12 minutes or until it turns golden in spots, stirring occasionally so it toasts evenly . Remove from the oven and let cool.

Indian Pudding Cheesecake
with black Walnut Crust and Rich Brandy Sauce

Fresh Peach Cheesecake
with Gingersnap-Hazelnut Crust and Peach Compote Topping

Red Currant Cheesecake
with Spiced Currant Sauce and Toasted Almonds

Irish Coffee Brownie Bottom Cheesecake
with Graham Cracker Crust and Irish Coffee Sauce

Arroz Con Dulce (Sweet Rice Pudding) Cheesecake
with Vanilla Wafer-Macadamia Nut Crust and Rum-Raisin Sauce

White Chocolate Cheesecake
with Cashew Crust and Cranberry-Cherry Sauce with Lime and Ginger

Mascarpone Cheesecake
with Toasted Pecan-Walnut Crust and Quince Compote

Chocolate Truffle Cheesecake
with Chocolate Wafer Crust and Hazelnut Topping

German Chocolate Cheesecake
with Chocolate Wafer Crust and Cognac Cherry Topping

Scottish Dundee Cheesecake
with Shortbread-English Walnut Crust and Traditional Hard Sauce

Eggnog Cheesecake
with Pecan Crust and Candied Kumquats

Triple Cheese Cheesecake
with Vanilla Wafer-Hazelnut Crust and Spiced Cranberry-Fig Relish

Chocolate-Bourbon Brownie Cheesecake
with Chocolate Wafer Crust and Bourbon Frosting

New Year's Day

As the holiday season comes to a close, and we celebrate the first day of a new year, we remember the prior year, make resolutions, plan for the year ahead, and just enjoy the last culinary indulgences of the season.

Start the year off right no matter if your New Year's Day plan is a football fest or a quiet recovery day with friends and family. A slice of delicate, velvety-smooth cheesecake will be just what everyone will be craving!

Start a New Year's Day tradition with an utterly decadent "Icon of Indulgence" that is eaten to celebrate the coming of a sweet year.

Happy New Year!

New Year's Day Cheesecake Suggestions

A Journey Into The Rich Lavish World of Cheesecakes

German Chocolate Cheesecake with Chocolate Wafer Crust and Cognac Cherry Sauce

Crust

1 1/2 c.   purchased chocolate wafer cookies, finely ground

1/4 c.   walnuts, finely chopped

1 tbsp.   all-purpose flour

6 tbsp.   unsalted butter, melted

Preheat oven to 375°F.

Lightly butter a 9-inch springform pan with 2 3/4-inch high sides. Wrap the outside of pan with 2 layers of heavy-duty foil.

In a food processor, pulse chocolate wafer cookies and walnuts until finely ground.

Transfer crumbs to a medium-size bowl and add flour; with a fork mix thoroughly. Stir in the melted butter and blend until evenly moistened and crumbs stick together when lightly pressed. Press the crust mixture onto bottom and 1 to 1 1/2 inches up the side of the cake pan and set aside.

Filling

4	8 oz. packages cream cheese, room temperature
1 1/4 c.	granulated sugar
1/4 tsp.	kosher salt
1 tsp.	pure vanilla extract
3 tbsp.	all-purpose flour
4	large eggs, room temperature
8	1 oz. squares German Sweet Chocolate, melted, slightly cooled
1/4 c.	sour cream

In a double boiler or bain-marie over gently simmering water, add chopped chocolate and 1/4 cup water and stir until chocolate is melted and smooth. Remove pan from heat and cool slightly.

In the bowl of a stand mixer fitted with the paddle attachment, beat the cream cheese on medium-high speed for 3 to 5 minutes or until velvety smooth. Add sugar, salt, vanilla extract, and flour and mix for an additional 2 to 3 minutes. Reduce mixer speed to low. Beat in the eggs one at a time until just blended, scraping down side of the bowl after each addition. Beat in melted chocolate and sour cream until evenly blended, making sure not to overmix after the eggs have been added.

Pour the filling over the crust in the prepared pan and spread evenly.

Place the springform pan in a large roasting pan with 2- to 3-inch high sides, and pour in enough boiling water to come halfway up the outside of the springform pan.

Bake the cheesecake for 1 hour to 1 hour and 15 minutes or until edge appears set and center jiggles when the pan is gently shaken. Remove springform pan from the oven and transfer to a wire rack, remove foil, and cool for 1 hour. Using a small knife or metal spatula, loosen crust from side of the pan, and continue to cool to room temperature for about 4 hours. Refrigerate for 8 hours or overnight.

Cognac Cherry Sauce

3/4 c.	cognac
1 3/4 c.	dried tart cherries (such as Balaton variety)
1/4	orange, peel and juice
1/4 tsp.	ground cinnamon
1 1/2 tsp.	arrowroot
1 tbsp.	cold water
1/4 tsp.	pure vanilla extract

In a medium-size saucepan, warm the cognac over low heat. Turn off the heat, add the cherries, and let them soak for 1 hour or until most of the liquid is absorbed.

Use a vegetable peeler to remove long strips of peel from a quarter of an orange, measure the juice squeezed from the orange and add enough water to make 3 tablespoons of liquid. Place juice, cinnamon, and orange peel into saucepan with cherries and cognac and bring to a boil.

In a cup, dissolve the arrowroot in the cold water and stir into saucepan. As soon as the sauce thickens, remove the pan from heat and stir in vanilla extract. Refrigerate sauce for 24 hours to allow flavors to marry.

Remove side of the springform pan from the chilled cheesecake and transfer to a serving dish. Cover entire top of the cheesecake with the cognac cherry sauce. Refrigerate for 1 hour or so before serving. Serve and enjoy!

Black Russian Brownie Cheesecake with Walnut Crust and Kahlúa Fudge Topping

Crust

1/2 c.	walnuts, finely ground
1 c.	graham cracker crumbs
1/4 c.	light brown sugar, packed
1/4 tsp.	ground cinnamon
5 tbsp.	unsalted butter, melted

Preheat oven to 350°F.

Lightly butter a 10-inch springform pan with 2 3/4-inch high sides; wrap outside of pan with 2 layers of heavy-duty foil.

In a medium-size bowl, combine walnuts, graham cracker crumbs, brown sugar, and cinnamon and mix with a fork until thoroughly combined. Stir in melted butter, and mix until crust mixture is evenly moistened. Transfer to the prepared pan, press over bottom and 1 to 1 1/2 inches up side of the springform pan and set aside.

Black Russian Brownies:

4 oz.	unsweetened chocolate (Lindt or Baker's), chopped
1 c.	unsalted butter (2 sticks)
1/4 tsp.	ground black pepper
4	large eggs, lightly beaten
1 1/2 c.	granulated sugar
1 1/2 tsp.	pure vanilla extract
1/3 c.	Kahlúa
2 tbsp.	vodka
1 1/3 c.	all-purpose flour
1/2 tsp.	kosher salt
1/4 tsp.	baking powder
1 c.	walnuts, coarsely chopped

In a small saucepan over low heat, melt chocolate and butter with pepper, stirring until smooth. Remove saucepan from heat and cool slightly.

Combine eggs, sugar, and vanilla in a large bowl and beat until thoroughly mixed. Stir in cooled chocolate mixture, Kahlúa, and vodka.

In another bowl, combine flour, salt, and baking powder; add chocolate mixture and stir until blended well. Stir in walnuts and spoon brownie mix into the prepared springform pan and spread evenly over bottom.

Bake for about 25 minutes or until a wooden toothpick inserted into the center comes out clean. Remove pan from the oven to a wire rack to cool and prepare filling.

Reduce oven temperature to 325°F.

Filling

3	8 oz. packages cream cheese, room temperature
1 c.	granulated sugar
1/2 tsp.	kosher salt
2 tsp.	pure vanilla extract
4	large eggs, room temperature
1/3 c.	sour cream

In the bowl of a stand mixer fitted with the paddle attachment, beat the cream cheese, sugar, salt, and vanilla extract on medium-high speed for 3 to 5 minutes, scraping down sides of the bowl several times, or until the mixture is smooth. Turn mixer speed to low and beat in the eggs one at a time until just blended, scraping down the side of the bowl after each addition. Add the sour cream and beat until just blended, being careful not to overmix once the eggs have been added.

Pour the filling over the brownie bottom in the prepared pan (filling will almost come to top of the pan).

Place springform pan in a large roasting pan with 2- to 3-inch high sides, and pour enough boiling water into roasting pan to come halfway up outside of the springform pan.

Bake 1 hour or until edge is set and center jiggles slightly when pan is gently shaken.

Remove springform pan from the water bath and transfer to a wire rack, remove foil, and cool for 1 hour. Run a small knife or metal spatula around rim of pan to loosen crust from side of pan. Cool to room temperature for about 4 hours. Cover and refrigerate for 8 hours or overnight.

Kahlúa Fudge:

6 oz.   semisweet chocolate (Lindt or Baker's), chopped

1 c.   unsalted butter (2 sticks)

1/4 c.   Kahlúa

1/4 c.   half and half

2 1/2 c.   confectioners' sugar

In a medium saucepan over medium heat, combine chopped chocolate, butter, Kahlúa, and half-and-half, stirring until chocolate melts.

Remove saucepan from heat; add confectioners' sugar and beat until frosting is cool and of spreading consistency.

Remove side of springform pan from cheesecake and evenly spread Kahlúa fudge topping on top of the cheesecake and sprinkle topping with walnut halves. Keep chilled until just before serving. Enjoy!

White Chocolate Grand Marnier Cheesecake with Macadamia Crust and Golden Nut Sauce

Crust

1 c.   macadamia nuts, toasted and finely chopped

1 c.   graham cracker crumbs

1/2 c.   granulated sugar

8 tbsp.   unsalted butter, melted

Preheat oven to 325°F.

Lightly butter a 10-inch springform pan with 2 3/4-inch high sides. Wrap the outside of pan with 2 layers of heavy-duty foil.

In a medium-size bowl, mix together chopped macadamia nuts, graham crackers, and sugar; stir in butter and mix together with a fork until mixture is evenly moistened and crumbs stick together when lightly pressed. Press the crumb mixture over bottom of springform pan and 1 to 1 1/2 inches up the side of pan and set aside.

Filling

1 lb.	good quality white chocolate (Lindt or Baker's), finely chopped
4	8 oz. packages cream cheese, room temperature
1 c.	granulated sugar
1/4 tsp.	kosher salt
4	large eggs, room temperature
1 c.	sour cream
1/2 c.	heavy cream
3 tbsp.	Grand Marnier

On the top container of a double boiler or bain-marie over barely simmering water, add 1/4 cup water and chopped chocolate and melt until smooth, stirring occasionally. Remove from over water and cool chocolate to lukewarm.

In the bowl of a stand mixer fitted with the paddle attachment, beat the cream cheese on medium-high speed for 3 to 5 minutes or until smooth. Gradually add sugar and salt, beat until fluffy for additional 2 to 3 minutes, occasionally scraping down side of bowl. Reduce mixer speed to low, add eggs one at a time and beat until just blended, scraping down side of bowl after each addition. Add the sour cream, heavy cream, and Grand Marnier and mix until just blended, careful to not overmix after eggs have been added.

Pour filling over crust and spread evenly over prepared pan.

Place springform pan in a large roasting pan with 2- to 3-inch high sides; pour enough boiling water into pan to come halfway up the outside of the springform pan.

Bake the cheesecake for 1 hour and 20 minutes or until the top begins to brown lightly, edges are set, and center moves slightly when the pan is gently shaken.

Remove springform pan from water bath and move to wire rack, remove foil, and cool for 1 hour. Loosen crust from side of pan with a small knife and continue to cool to room temperature for about 3 to 4 hours. Cover and refrigerate for 8 hours or overnight before serving.

Chef's tip: Cheesecake can be made 2 days ahead; cover and keep refrigerated.

Golden Nut Sauce

8 tbsp.	unsalted butter
1 1/4 c.	light brown sugar, packed
1/4 c.	water
1/2 c.	heavy cream
2 tsp.	fresh lemon juice
4 tbsp.	apricot jam
1 c.	toasted macadamia nuts, coarsely chopped

In a medium saucepan, melt the butter over low heat; add the brown sugar and water, stir until sugar has dissolved. Increase the heat to medium-high and bring to a boil, add cream and lemon juice while constantly stirring. Cook the sauce for 2 to 3 minutes longer, remove saucepan from the heat and keep warm.

In a small saucepan, warm the apricot jam over low heat until liquid. Strain through a fine-mesh strainer.

Brush the top of the cheesecake with the jam. Cover the top of the cake with an even layer of toasted macadamia nuts. Chill until just before serving.

Spoon nut sauce over sliced cheesecake and serve. Enjoy!

Bruce A. Williamson

Canadian Orange Cheesecake with Gingersnap-Pecan Crust and Riesling-Kumquat Sauce

Cheesecake recipe inspired by: *Canadian Living Magazine*, December 2003; Riesling-Kumquat Sauce inspired by: Samantha Seneviratne .

Crust

1 1/2 c.   purchased gingersnap cookies, finely ground

1/2 c.   pecans, finely chopped

1/4 c.   light brown sugar, packed

2 tbsp.   crystallized ginger, chopped (optional)

4 tbsp.   unsalted butter, melted

Preheat oven to 350°F.

Lightly butter a 9-inch springform pan with 2 3/4-inch high sides and wrap outside of pan with 2 layers of heavy-duty foil.

In a food processor, pulse gingersnap cookies and pecans until finely ground.

Transfer mixture to a medium-size bowl, add the brown sugar and crystallized ginger and combine thoroughly with a fork. Add the melted butter and combine until evenly moistened and crumbs stick together when lightly pressed. Press crust mixture over bottom and 1 to 1 1/2 inches up the side of the prepared pan.

Bake crust for 10 to 12 minutes or until set and lightly browned. Transfer to a wire rack and cool completely.

Reduce oven temperature to 325°F.

Filling

2	8 oz. packages cream cheese, room temperature
1	16 oz. container cottage cheese, room temperature
3/4 c.	granulated sugar
2	large eggs, room temperature
1/2 c.	sour cream
1 tbsp.	orange zest, finely chopped
2 tbsp.	all-purpose flour
1 tsp.	pure vanilla extract

In the bowl of a stand mixer fitted with the paddle attachment, beat the cream cheese, cottage cheese, and sugar on medium-high speed until smooth, scraping down side of bowl occasionally. On low speed, add the eggs one at a time and beat until just blended, scraping down the bowl after each addition. Stir in the sour cream, orange zest, flour, and vanilla extract and mix until just blended. Do not overmix filling after eggs have been added.

Pour filling over crust in the prepared pan and gently tap springform pan on the countertop to remove air bubbles from the filling.

Set the springform pan into a large roasting pan, and pour in enough boiling water to come halfway up the outside of the springform pan.

Bake for 50 minutes to 1 hour and 5 minutes or until edge is set and center jiggles slightly when the pan is gently shaken.

Remove springform pan from water bath and transfer to a wire rack, remove foil, and cool for 1 hour. Using a small knife or metal spatula, cut around edge of pan to loosen crust from the side of the pan. Continue to cool cheesecake to room temperature, about 4 hours.

Chef's tip: Cheesecake can be made up to 2 days ahead. Cover and refrigerate in pan.

Riesling-Kumquat Sauce

2 1/2 c.	Riesling, semisweet or sweet
2/3 c.	clover honey
1/2 c.	granulated sugar
3	1/4" thick slices fresh ginger, peeled
1	cinnamon stick
1	vanilla bean, seeded
1/4 c.	water
2 1/2 c.	kumquats, 1/4" thick slices and seeded

In a medium-size saucepan over high heat, combine the Riesling, honey, sugar, ginger, cinnamon stick, vanilla seeds, vanilla pod, and water and bring to a boil. Add the kumquat slices and reduce the heat to medium-low. Cook the kumquats for 25 to 30 minutes or until they are tender and translucent and the liquid is syrupy. Cool to room temperature.

Remove side of springform pan and transfer the cheesecake to a serving platter. To serve, slice the cheesecake and top with kumquats and drizzle with syrup. Enjoy!

Chef's tip: Suggested wines for kumquat sauce include Viu Manent-Late Harvest Semillon (Chile) or Late Harvest, full-bodied, rich, Riesling.

White Russian Cheesecake with Toasted Black Walnut Crust and White Russian Sauce

Crust

1 1/2 c.   purchased shortbread cookies, finely ground

1/2 c.   black walnuts, toasted

1/4 c.   granulated sugar

5 tbsp.   unsalted butter, melted

Preheat oven to 350°F.

Lightly butter a 9-inch springform pan with 2 3/4-inch high sides. Wrap the outside of pan with 2 layers of heavy-duty foil. Set aside.

In a food processor, pulse shortbread cookies and toasted black walnuts until finely ground.

Transfer the mixture to a medium-size bowl, add the sugar and with a fork, combine thoroughly. Add the melted butter to the crumbs and blend until evenly moistened and mixture sticks together when lightly pressed. Press mixture over bottom and 1 to 1 1/2 inches up the side of the prepared springform pan.

Bake the crust for 10 to 12 minutes or until set and golden brown. Transfer crust to a wire rack and cool completely.

Reduce the oven temperature to 325°F.

Filling

4	8 oz. packages cream cheese, room temperature
1 1/3 c.	granulated sugar
1/2 tsp.	kosher salt
5	large eggs, room temperature
1 tsp.	pure vanilla extract
2/3 c.	sour cream
1/4 c.	Kahlúa
2 tbsp.	vodka

In the bowl of a stand mixer fitted with the paddle attachment, beat the cream cheese on medium-high speed for 3 to 5 minutes. Gradually add the sugar and salt and continue to beat the mixture for 2 to 3 minutes more, scraping down the side of the bowl several times or until it is smooth and creamy. Turn the mixer to low speed and beat in the eggs one at a time until just blended, scraping down the side of the bowl after each addition. Beat in the vanilla, sour cream, Kahlúa, and vodka until just blended, careful not to overmix once the eggs have been added.

Pour the filling over the crust in the prepared pan.

Place the springform pan into a large roasting pan with 2- to 3-inch high sides. Place the roasting pan into the oven and pour in enough boiling water to come halfway up the outside of the springform pan.

Bake the cheesecake for 1 hour and 30 minutes to 1 hour and 45 minutes or until the edge is set and the center jiggles when the pan is gently shaken.

Remove the cheesecake from the oven to a wire rack, remove foil, and let cool for 1 hour. Using a small knife or metal spatula, cut around edge of the pan to loosen crust from the side of the pan. Continue to cool to room temperature for about 4 hours. Chill the cheesecake 6 to 8 hours or overnight in the pan.

White Russian Sauce

10 oz.	heavy cream
1/2	vanilla bean, seeded
1/3 c.	Kahlúa
3 tbsp.	vodka
6 oz.	good quality white chocolate, chopped (Lindt or Baker's)

Pour the heavy cream into a small saucepan. Split the vanilla bean lengthwise and remove the seeds with a small knife. Add the seeds to the cream along with the pod and bring to a boil over medium-high heat.

Remove the pan from the heat, cover, and let stand for 10 minutes. Strain the mixture through a fine-mesh strainer.

In a separate bowl, add the chopped white chocolate, reheat the cream and pour over the chocolate and let stand for 2 minutes. Then stir until melted and mixture is smooth. Set aside and keep warm.

Remove the side of the springform pan from the cheesecake and transfer to a serving dish. Slice the cheesecake, top with sauce, and serve. Enjoy!

Eggnog Cheesecake with Pecan Crust and Candied Kumquats

Crust

1 c.	pecans, finely chopped
1 c.	graham cracker crumbs
1/2 c.	granulated sugar
8 tbsp.	unsalted butter, melted

Preheat oven to 350°F.

Lightly butter a 10-inch springform pan with 2 3/4-inch high sides, and wrap the outside of the pan with 2 layers of heavy-duty foil.

In a medium-size bowl, combine pecans, graham cracker crumbs, and sugar and mix until thoroughly combined. Add butter, and mix with a fork until mixture is evenly moistened and sticks together when lightly pressed. Press the mixture over the bottom and 1 to 1 1/2 inches up the side of the prepared pan; set aside.

Filling

4	8 oz. packages cream cheese, room temperature
1 c.	granulated sugar
1 tsp.	pure vanilla extract
1/2 tsp.	ground nutmeg
3	large eggs, room temperature
1 1/2 c.	eggnog

In the bowl of a stand mixer fitted with the paddle attachment, beat the cream cheese and sugar on medium-high speed for 3 to 5 minutes or until smooth and fluffy; scrape down the side of the bowl several times. Beat in the vanilla and nutmeg and continue to mix for an additional 2 to 3 minutes. Turn the mixer to low and beat in the eggs one at a time until just blended; scrape down the side of the bowl after each addition. Add the eggnog and mix until just blended, making sure not to overmix after the eggs have been added.

Pour the filling over the crust in the prepared pan, and tap several times on the countertop to release any air bubbles from the filling.

Place the springform pan into a large roasting pan with 2- to 3-inch high sides and pour enough boiling water into the roasting pan to come halfway up the outside of the springform pan.

Bake for 1 hour to 1 hour and 10 minutes or until the edge is set and the center wobbles when the pan is gently shaken.

Remove the springform pan from the oven to a wire rack, remove foil, and cool for 1 hour. Using a small knife or metal spatula, cut around the rim to loosen crust from the side of the pan. Continue to cool to room temperature for about 3 to 4 hours. Refrigerate the cheesecake in the pan for 8 hours or overnight.

Candied Kumquats

2 c.	granulated sugar
2 c.	water
1	vanilla bean, seeded
25	medium kumquats, thinly sliced, seeds removed

In a medium-size saucepan over medium-high heat, combine the sugar, water, vanilla bean seeds, and bean pod and bring to a boil, stirring occasionally until sugar dissolves. Reduce heat to low, add kumquat slices and simmer for 20 to 25 minutes or until slices are translucent.

Remove saucepan from the heat; with a slotted spoon remove kumquat slices from the syrup and cool. Return saucepan to heat and bring back to a boil and reduce syrup by half.

Arrange kumquat slices on top of the cheesecake. Refrigerate the cheesecake and syrup until just before serving. Drizzle slices with syrup and serve. Enjoy!

Chef's tip: Candied kumquats and syrup can be made 2 days ahead.

Mascarpone Cheesecake with Black Walnut Crust and Inebriated Fig Topping

Inebriated Figs

6 oz.	Calimyrna figs
6 oz.	black mission figs
1 tbsp.	light brown sugar, packed
1 c.	orange juice
1/4 c.	brandy or cognac
1	bay leaf
3	whole cloves
1	cinnamon stick

In a medium-size saucepan, combine all ingredients and bring to a boil over medium heat. Reduce heat to low, and simmer for 20 minutes or until figs are plump and the liquid has reduced by 2/3.

Remove fig mixture from heat and cool to room temperature; cover and refrigerate overnight.

Chef's tip: Inebriated figs can be made up to 1 week ahead, keep tightly covered and refrigerated.

Crust

1 c.	black walnuts, finely chopped and toasted
1/2 c.	graham cracker crumbs
1/4 c.	granulated sugar
5 tbsp.	unsalted butter, melted

Preheat oven to 325°F.

Lightly butter a 9-inch springform pan with 2 3/4-inch high sides and wrap the outside of pan with 2 layers of heavy-duty foil. Set aside.

In a food processor, finely grind toasted walnuts.

Transfer ground nuts to a medium-size bowl, add graham cracker crumbs and sugar; combine thoroughly with a fork. Add melted butter to the mixture and combine until evenly moistened and crumbs stick together when lightly pressed. Press mixture over bottom of pan and 1 to 1 1/2 inches up side of the cake pan and set aside.

Filling

2	8 oz. packages cream cheese, room temperature
2	8 oz. containers mascarpone cheese, room temperature
1 1/4 c.	granulated sugar
	Pinch kosher salt
1 tsp.	pure vanilla extract

4	large eggs, room temperature
1 tsp.	brandy (optional)
1/2 c.	sour cream

In the bowl of a stand mixer fitted with the paddle attachment, beat the cream cheese, mascarpone cheese, sugar, and salt for 3 to 5 minutes or until velvety smooth, scraping down the side of the bowl occasionally. Add vanilla extract and blend for another 2 to 3 minutes. On low speed, add the eggs one at a time and mix until just blended; scrape down the side of bowl after each addition. Add brandy and sour cream and mix until just blended, making sure not to overmix after the eggs have been added.

Pour filling over crust in prepared pan, and tap gently on countertop several times to remove air bubbles from the filling.

Place the springform pan in a large roasting pan with 2- to 3-inch high sides, and pour enough boiling water into the roasting pan to come halfway up the outside of the springform pan.

Bake cheesecake for 1 hour and 15 minutes to 1 hour and 30 minutes or until edge is set and center wiggles when the pan is gently shaken.

Remove springform pan from the oven and transfer to a wire rack, remove foil, and cool for 1 hour. Using a small knife or metal spatula, cut around edge of pan to loosen crust from side of pan. Cool to room temperature for about 4 hours. Loosely cover and refrigerate for 8 hours or overnight.

When ready to serve, remove side of springform pan from cheesecake and cover the top of the cake with inebriated figs and drizzle with remaining syrup. Serve and enjoy!

Triple Cheese Cheesecake with Vanilla Wafer-Hazelnut Crust and Spiced Cranberry-Fig Relish

Crust

1 c.   purchased vanilla wafer cookies, finely chopped

1 c.   toasted hazelnuts, finely chopped

1/4 c.   granulated sugar

6 tbsp.   unsalted butter, melted

Preheat oven to 325°F.

Lightly butter a 9-inch springform pan with 2 3/4-inch high sides. Wrap outside of cake pan with 2 layers of heavy-duty foil.

In a food processor add vanilla wafers and toasted hazelnuts; grind until finely chopped.

Transfer crumbs to a medium-size bowl, add sugar and combine thoroughly with a fork. Add melted butter to the crumb mixture, and blend until evenly moistened and crumbs stick together when lightly pressed. Transfer crust mixture to the prepared pan and press crumbs firmly over the bottom and 1 to 1 1/2 inches up the side of the pan; set aside.

Filling

2	8 oz. packages cream cheese, room temperature
1	8 oz. container mascarpone cheese, room temperature
1	8 oz. package fresh goat cheese, room temperature
3/4 c.	granulated sugar
1/2	vanilla bean, seeded
4	large eggs, room temperature
3 tbsp.	Frangelico (hazelnut liqueur)
1/2 c.	sour cream

In the bowl of an electric stand mixer fitted with the paddle attachment on medium-high speed, beat the cream cheese, mascarpone, and goat cheese for 3 to 5 minutes or until smooth and well-combined, occasionally scraping down the side of the bowl. Add sugar and vanilla seeds and beat for 2 to 3 minutes more or until smooth and fluffy . With mixer speed on low, add the eggs one at a time and beat until just blended; scrape down the side of the bowl after each addition. Add Frangelico and sour cream and mix until just blended, being careful not to overmix after the eggs have been added.

Pour filling over the crust in the prepared pan, and tap gently on the countertop to remove any air bubbles from the filling.

Place the springform pan in a large roasting pan with 2- to 3-inch high sides, and pour enough boiling water into the roasting pan to come halfway up the outside of the springform pan.

Bake for 1 hour and 10 minutes or until edges look set and center wobbles when the pan is gently shaken.

Remove the cheesecake from the oven and transfer to a wire rack, remove foil, and cool for 1 hour. Using a small knife or metal spatula, cut around edge of the pan to loosen crust from the side. Cool cake to room temperature for about 4 hours. Cover and refrigerate cheesecake for 8 hours or overnight before serving.

Spiced Cranberry-Fig Relish

1	12 oz. bag fresh cranberries
1 1/2 c.	dried Calimyrna figs, quartered
1 1/4 c.	water
3/4 c.	granulated sugar
1/2 tsp.	five-spice powder
1 tsp.	ground cinnamon
1/4 tsp.	ground cloves
1/4 tsp.	ground allspice
1/8 tsp.	ground pepper

In a medium-size saucepan, combine all the ingredients and bring to a boil over medium-high heat. Reduce the heat to medium-low and boil for 10 to 12 minutes or until cranberries have popped, stirring mixture occasionally. Remove saucepan from the heat and cool relish completely. Cover and refrigerate.

Remove side of springform pan from the cheesecake and transfer to a serving plate. Spoon relish over top of chilled cheesecake and spread evenly, covering entire top of the cheesecake. Slice, serve, and enjoy!

Chef's tip: Spiced cranberry-fig relish can be made 1 to 2 days ahead; tightly cover and refrigerate.

Honey Ricotta Cheesecake with Limequat Buttercream Topping

Recipe inspired by Giada De Laurentiis

Crust

1 1/2 c.   biscotti, finely ground (2 packages)

1/8 c.   ea. almonds and walnuts, finely chopped

1/4 c.   granulated sugar

1/4 tsp.   anise extract

6 tbsp.   unsalted butter, melted

Preheat oven to 350°F.

Lightly butter a 9-inch springform pan with 2 3/4-inch high sides. Wrap the outside of pan with 2 layers of heavy-duty foil.

In a food processor, finely grind biscotti.

Transfer crumbs to a medium-size bowl, add 1/8 cup almonds, 1/8 cup walnuts, and sugar; mix to combine. Add anise to the melted butter and stir to combine. Add butter to crumb mixture and with a fork, blend until crumbs are evenly moistened. Press the crumb mixture over the bottom of the prepared pan and 1 to 1 1/2 inches up the side of the pan.

Bake the crust for 12 to 15 minutes or until set and golden. Cool the crust on a wire rack completely.

Filling

1	16 oz. container whole milk ricotta, drained
2	8 oz. packages cream cheese, room temperature
3/4 c.	granulated sugar
1/4 c.	clover honey
1 tbsp.	lemon zest
1 1/2 tsp.	pure vanilla extract
4	large eggs, room temperature

In the mixing bowl of a stand mixer fitted with the paddle attachment, beat ricotta cheese until smooth. Add cream cheese and sugar and beat on medium-high speed for 3 to 5 minutes or until the mixture is smooth and fluffy, scraping down the side of bowl several times. Add honey and zest and continue to beat for an additional 2 to 3 minutes. Turn the mixer to low and beat in the eggs one at a time until just blended, scraping down the side of the bowl after each addition. Beat in vanilla until just blended; do not overmix once eggs have been added.

Pour the filling over the crust in the prepared pan.

Place the springform pan in a large roasting pan. Pour enough boiling water into the roasting pan to come halfway up the outside of the springform pan.

Bake the cheesecake about 1 hour and 5 minutes or until the edge is firm and the center appears nearly set when the pan is gently shaken.

Remove springform pan from the oven and transfer to a wire rack, remove foil, and cool for 1 hour. Using a small knife or metal spatula, cut around edge of pan to loosen crust from side of pan. Cool to room temperature for about 4 hours. Loosely cover and refrigerate for 8 hours or overnight.

Chef's tip: To strain ricotta, place the ricotta in a fine-mesh strainer or a cheesecloth lined strainer that has been suspended over a bowl, cover and place in the refrigerator to drain for several hours or overnight.

Limequat Buttercream

1 c.   granulated sugar

3 tbsp.   water

             Pinch of kosher salt

1/4 c.   heavy cream

4 tbsp.   unsalted butter, cubed

2 oz.   cream cheese, cut into 1-inch cubes

5 tbsp.   fresh limequat juice

Boil the sugar, water, and salt in a medium saucepan over high heat for about 5 minutes, gently swirling occasionally to prevent scorching. Whisk in cream and the butter pieces (mixture will bubble furiously; keep whisking). Boil for 2 minutes more.

Transfer buttercream to the bowl of a stand mixer and whip on high speed for 8 to 10 minutes or until side of the bowl is cool to the touch and buttercream is thick; scrape sides of the bowl as needed. Add cream cheese one cube at a time until buttercream is smooth. Add limequat juice and mix until just blended.

Spread buttercream topping onto cooled cheesecake; cover and chill till just before serving. Enjoy!

Chef's tip: A limequat is a cross between a key lime and a kumquat; both the peel and flesh can be eaten. Slightly acidic and spicy, limequats are yellow in color with a greenish tint. The oval fruit has a shiny, thin, sweet-tasting skin that encases a bittersweet flesh and small edible seeds. Limequats are very juicy. Limequats season typically begins in November.

Caramelized Limequat (optional topping)

3/4 lb.	limequats, about 10 to 12
1/2 c.	granulated sugar
1/2 c.	water
	Pinch of kosher salt
2 tbsp.	limequat juice

Slice limequats about 1/8-inch thick, removing any seeds.

In a medium-size skillet over medium heat, boil sugar and water until sugar dissolves and liquid thickens. Lower the heat and add the limequat slices. Stir mixture occasionally and cook for about 15 to 20 minutes or until the rind becomes tender. Cool caramelized fruit slightly.

Cover the top of the cheesecake with fruit, cover and chill until just before serving.

Bruce A. Williamson

Chocolate-Bourbon Brownie Cheesecake with Chocolate Wafer Crust and Bourbon Frosting

Crust

1 1/2 c.   purchased chocolate wafer cookies, finely ground

1 tbsp.   all-purpose flour

6 tbsp.   unsalted butter, melted

Preheat the oven to 350°F.

Lightly butter a 10-inch springform pan with 2 3/4-inch high sides, and wrap the outside of the pan with 2 layers of heavy-duty foil.

In a medium-size bowl, combine chocolate wafer crumbs and flour; mix thoroughly with a fork. Stir in melted butter, and blend until mixture is evenly moistened and crumbs stick together when lightly pressed. Press crumb mixture over bottom and 1 to 1 1/2 inches up side of the prepared pan. Set aside.

Brownie Filling

1/2 c.	granulated sugar
5 tbsp.	unsalted butter, cubed
2 tbsp.	water
1 c.	semi-sweet chocolate pieces
2	large eggs, room temperature
1 tsp.	pure vanilla extract
3/4 c.	all-purpose flour
1/4 tsp.	baking soda
1/4 tsp.	kosher salt
1 c.	cooking apples, cored, peeled, and finely chopped
1/2 c.	pecans, toasted and coarsely chopped
3 tbsp.	bourbon

In a medium saucepan, combine sugar, butter, and water. Cook and stir over medium heat just until boiling. Remove pan from heat.

Stir in chocolate pieces until melted. Add the eggs and vanilla, beating with a wooden spoon until just combined. Stir in flour, baking soda, and salt until blended. Stir in apples and pecans. Pour batter over crust in prepared pan, spreading evenly.

Bake about 25 minutes or until toothpick inserted near the center comes out clean. Place pan on a wire rack. Brush top of hot brownies with bourbon. Cool slightly on wire rack.

Filling

4	8 oz. packages cream cheese, room temperature
1 c.	granulated sugar
4	large eggs, room temperature
2 tsp.	pure vanilla extract
1/2 c.	sour cream

In the bowl of a stand mixer fitted with the paddle attachment, beat the cream cheese and sugar on medium-high speed for 3 to 5 minutes or until just smooth, scraping down side of the bowl several times. Reduce the mixer to low speed, and add the eggs one at a time and beat until just blended; scrape down the bowl after each addition. Add vanilla and sour cream and mix until just blended; make sure not to overmix after the eggs have been added. Pour filling over brownies.

Place the springform pan in a large roasting pan with 2- to 3-inch high sides, and pour enough boiling water into the roasting pan to come halfway up the outside of the springform pan.

Bake for 50 to 55 minutes or until edge is set and center jiggles when pan is gently shaken.

Transfer springform pan to a wire rack, remove foil, and cool for 1 hour. Run a small knife or metal spatula around rim of the pan to loosen crust from side of the pan. Continue to cool to room temperature for about 4 hours. Refrigerate for 8 hours or overnight in pan.

Bourbon Frosting

3 tbsp.	unsalted butter, softened
1 1/2 c.	confectioners' sugar
1 tbsp.	bourbon
1/4 tsp.	pure vanilla extract
	milk, as needed

In a medium-size bowl, beat softened butter with an electric mixer on medium-high speed for 30 to 45 seconds. Gradually add powdered sugar, beating well. Mix in bourbon and vanilla until thoroughly mixed. If necessary, beat in 1 teaspoon of milk at a time to make frosting a spreadable consistency.

Spread frosting evenly over top of cheesecake and keep chilled until just before serving. Slice, serve, and enjoy!

The Perfect Complement: Cheesecake and Wine

*H*oliday desserts can be improved with wine. Ever notice your kitchen is the room where everyone gathers when entertaining friends and family? This is particularly true during the holidays where the meal's enticing aromas are sure to attract a crowd.

The role of dessert is to top off a great meal. Pairing a wine with your favorite cheesecake is a special treat. Like a good marriage, wine and cheesecake were meant for each other. Each enhances and strengthens the experience. So why is it so daunting to try to pair cheesecakes with wines? Rumor has it that there are hefty lists of rules that require strict adherence in order to obtain the perfect wine and cheesecake pairing. That said, the simplest rule is this; the wine should be as sweet or slightly sweeter than the cheesecake; so the sweeter the cheesecake, the sweeter the wine, with enough acidity for balance.

What is the best wine to go with your unique richly-flavored creamy cheesecake? I've listed some suggested pairings with each of the recipes in this cookbook. Toast your family and friends with any (or all) of these perfect matches!

Thanksgiving

Cheesecake

Wine

Pumpkin Mousse Cheesecake
with Gingersnap-Pecan Crust and Caramel
Buttercream with Bacon and Sea Salt Topping

Gonzales Byass - Pedro Ximénez Sherry

Indian Pudding Cheesecake
with Black Walnut Crust and Maple
Buttercream Topping

Quady Electra (orange Muscay)

Caramelized Apple-Ginger Cheesecake
with Gingersnap-Pecan Crust and Apple Topping

Quarts de Chaume - late harvest Chenin Blanc
Coterux du Layon - late harvest Chenin Blanc

Decadent Chocolate-Cranberry Cheesecake
with Chocolate Wafer Crust and Cranberry
Compote Filling with Simmered Orange Topping

Rosenblum Cellars
Désirée (chocolate dessert wine)

Fresh Peach Cheesecake
with Gingersnap-Hazelnut Crust and Peach
Compote Topping

Gewürztraminer

White Chocolate Cheesecake
with Cashew Crust and Cranberry-Pomegranate
Sauce

Branchetto d'Acqui

A Journey Into The Rich Lavish World of Cheesecakes

Red Currant Cheesecake
with Spiced Currant Sauce and Toasted Almonds

Demi Sec Champagne
Branchetto d'Aqui
Sparkling Wine topped with PAMA
Kir (classic French apéritif

Sweet Potato Cheesecake
with Black Walnut Crust and Maple Buttercream
Topping

Demi Sec Champagne

Mascarpone Cheesecake
with Biscotti Crust and Spicy Peach Sauce

Gewürztraminer

Vanilla Bean Cheesecake
with Triple-Nut Filling and Vanilla Sauce

Moscato d'Oro

Irish Coffee Brownie Bottom Cheesecake
with Graham Cracker Crust and Irish Coffee
Sauce

California rich Zinfandel

Orange Cheesecake
with Cashew Crust and Cranberry-Kumquat
Compote

Quady Essensia (orange Muscat)

Chocolate-Bourbon-Pecan Cheesecake
with Vanilla Wafer Crust and Vanilla Pecan
Sauce

California Zinfandel Port

Christmas

Arroz Con Dulce (Sweet Rice Pudding)   Sauternes
Cheesecake
with Vanilla Wafer-Maccdamia Nut Crust
and Rum Raisin Sauce

Indian Pudding Cheesecake   Tawny Port
with Black Walnut Crust and Rich Brandy Sauce

White Chocolate Cheesecake   Kirsch Eau de Vie
with Cashew Crust and Cranberry- Cherry
Sauce with Lime and Ginger

Caramelized Apple-Ginger Cheesecake   Moscato d'Asti
with Gingersnap-Pecan Crust and Brandy
Caramel Sauce

Scottish Dundee Cheesecake   Gewürztraminer
with Shortbread-English Walnut Crust and
Scottish Orange Marmalade Topping
Blackcurrant Cheesecake   Quady Elysium (dark black Muscat)
with Graham Cracker-English Walnut Crust   Kir Royal (champagne topped with Crème de
and Blackcurrant Glaze   Cassis)

Eggnog Cheesecake   Landmark Lorenzo Chardonnay
with Cashew Crust and Brandy Buttercream
Topping

A Journey Into The Rich Lavish World of Cheesecakes

Mascarpone Cheesecake
with Toasted Pecan-Walnut Crust and Quince
Compote

Quincy Wine
Sancerre Wine
Vouvray (Chenin Blanc)

Clementine-Date Cheesecake
with Spicy Date Filling and Poached Clementines
in a Grand Marnier Sauce

Muscat
Moscato d'Oro

Greek Cheesecake
with Baked Fig Filling and Poached
Fig Topping

Lighter to Richer sweet style Madeira
Mavrodaphne
Muscat de Patras

Chocolate Truffle Cheesecake
with Chocolate Wafer Crust and Hazelnut
Topping

Oloroso Sherry
Pedro Ximénez Sherry

Bourbon Cheesecake
with Pecan-Date Crust and Bourbon-Molasses
Buttercream

Aged Tawny Port (10 to 20 Year old)

Rum-Raisin Cheesecake
with Rum-Pecan Caramel Sauce

Any Sparkling Wine topped with Coconut
Vodka

New Year's Day

German Chocolate Cheesecake
with Chocolate Wafer Crust and Cognac
Cherry Sauce

Maderia
10 year old Malmsey

Black Russian Brownie Cheesecake
with Walnut Crust and Kahúa Fudge Topping

Cabernet Sauvignon
Young Beaujolais

White Chocolate Grand Marnier Cheesecake
with Macadamia Nut Crust and Golden
Nut Sauce

Aged White Burgundy

Scottish Dundee Cheesecake
with Shortbread-English Walnut Crust and
Traditional Hard Sauce

Small Batch Bourbon

Canadian Orange Cheesecake
with Gingersnap-Pecan Crust and Riesling-
Kumquat Sauce

Alsatian Riesling
Viu Manent - late harvest Sémillon

White Chocolate Cheesecake
with Cashew Crust and Honey-Lemon
Cranberry Sauce with Rosemary

Asbach Uralt

White Russian Cheesecake
with Toasted Black Walnut Crust and White
Russian Sauce

Choco Vine (French cabernet subtly combined
with rich dark chocolate)

A Journey Into The Rich Lavish World of Cheesecakes

Eggnog Cheesecake
with Pecan Crust and Candied Kumquats

Condrieu Wine (France, Rhone Valley)

Mascarpone Cheesecake
with Black Walnut Crust and Inebriated Fig
Topping

Young Beaujolais

Triple Cheese Cheesecake
with Vanilla Wafer-Hazelnut Crust and Spiced
Cranberry-Fig Relish

Light-full bodied Pinot Noir

Orange Cheesecake
with Cashew Crust and Orange Liqueur Sauce

Orange Muscat

Honey Ricotta Cheesecake
with Limequat Buttercream Topping

French Coteaux d'Aix-en-Provence (Rosé Wine)
Rich, round French Rosé from Rhone the Valley

Chocolate-Bourbon Brownie Cheesecake
with Chocolate Wafer Crust and Bourbon
Frosting

Marenco Brachetto d'Acqui
Ruby Port

Online Sources

*T*hese days, you can find almost anything you want by searching the Internet. Products that are not available in local stores are less expensive when purchased online, or seasonal items that are not available locally can be purchased online. Here are a variety of online sources that can supply your holiday cheesecake-making needs.

Avanti Savoia
Gourmet honey from around the world
www.avantisavoia.com/gourmet-honey
1-800-213-2927

Browning's Honey Co.
Premium clover, orange blossom, and flavored honey
www.browningshoney.com
(208) 523-3692 ext. 14

Buy Exotic Fruits
Fresh tree ripened kumquats
www.buyexoticfruits.com/kumquats.html
California 714-656-4148   New York 718-577-1394
New Jersey 201-204-9451   Seattle 206-455-9989

Cherry Bay Orchards
Dried Montmorency and Balaton Cherries
www.cherrybayorchards.com
231-941-433

Hale Groves
Hand-picked, fresh from the grove clementines
www.halegroves.com/clementines
800-562-4502

Local Harvest
Find locally grown currants, honey, kumquats, and quinces
www.localharvest.org/ (enter product)

Nuts.com
Variety of premium nuts, dried cherries, dates, and figs
www.nuts.com/nuts
www.nuts.com/driedfruit
800-558-6887

Superior Nut Company
Large selection of bulk nuts, dates, and figs
www.superiornutstore.com
800-295-4093

Top Vanilla
Premium Madagascar bourbon vanilla beans at ridiculously low prices (10 vanilla beans for $7.99 + shipping)
www.topvanilla.com

Brits
Source for Scottish marmalades (Keiller Dundee Orange Marmalade and Duerr's 1881 Original)
brits@britusa.com
Mail order: 888-382-7487

"Your" Local Product Sources

*A*s I have mentioned in the beginning of this book, being a chef myself, I am committed to the principle of "market cooking," the dedication to the use of the finest, sustainable ingredients that are seasonal and produced from local sources.

Working with the State of Connecticut Department of Agriculture, my original intention was to comprise a list of Connecticut-grown and produced ingredients that can be used in the recipes in this book.

But in the course of researching online sources for products on the Internet, I came upon a website that was used as a link for several of the products being researched. This website uses a product description in conjunction with your zip code or city and state where you live. The results of the search indicate farms, farmers markets, grocery/co-ops, and online stores where items can be purchased from local growers and producers.

Localharvest.org provides a number of services and venues to obtain locally grown, sustainable, and organic fruits and vegetables grown closest to you.

By purchasing your ingredients locally, it preserves the environment, it is fresher than anything in a supermarket, it is tastier and more nutritious, and it is good for your local economy. Buying direct from family farmers helps them to stay in business.

So give localharvest.org a try and create your own local product sources list.

Connecticut Grown Product Sources

Belltown Hill Orchards
483 Matson Hill Road, South Glastonbury, CT 06073
Phone: 860-633-2789 Email: belltownorchard@snet.net
Products: apples (Honeycrisp, Jonagold), peaches, and pumpkins

Blue Hills Orchard
141 Blue Hills Road, Wallingford Center, CT 06492-4318
Phone: 203-269-3189 Email: eric@bluehillsorchard.com
Products: apples (Honeycrisp, Jonagold) and local honey

Lyman Orchards
32 Reeds Gap Road, Middlefield, CT 06455
Phone: 860-349-1793 Email: jlyman3@lymanorchards.com
Products: apples (Honeycrisp, Jonagold) and online shopping

Rogers Orchards – Shuttle Meadow Farm
336 Long Bottom Road, Southington, CT 06489
Phone: 860-229-4240
Products: apples (Honeycrisp), peaches, honey, and maple syrup

Averill Farm
250 Calhoun Street, Washington Depot, CT 06794
Phone: 860-868-2777 Email: averillfarm@sbcglobal.net
Products: apples (Jonagold), honey, maple syrup, and pumpkins

Easy Pickin's Orchard
46 Bailey Road, Enfield, CT 06082
Phone: 860-763-3276 Email: farmer@easypickinorchard.net
Products: apples (Jonagold), peaches, and honey

Hickory Hill Orchard
363 South Meriden Road, Cheshire, CT 06410
Phone: 203-272-0181
Products: apples (Honeycrisp, Jonagold), peaches, and maple syrup

March Farm
160 Munger Lane, Bethlehem, CT 06751
Phone: 203-266-7721 Email: marchfarms@marchfarms.com
Products: apples (Honeycrisp, Jonagold), peaches, honey, and pumpkins

B.W. Bishop and Sons, Inc.
1355 Boston Post Road, Gilford, CT 06437-2399
Phone: 203-453-2338 Email: farminfo@bishopsorchard.com
Products: apples (Honeycrisp, Jonagold), peaches, and pumpkins. Bishop's Orchard's Farm Winery features award-winning wines, as well as a collection of Connecticut wines.

Aspetuck Valley Apple Barn
714 Black Root Turnpike, Easton, CT 06612
Phone: 203-268-9033
Products: maple syrup and local honey

Peter Draghi Farm
379 Scantic Road, East Windsor, CT 06088
Phone: 860-282-9063
Products: apples (Honeycrisp), peaches, and local honey

Woodstock Orchards
494 Connecticut 169, Woodstock, CT 06281-3041
Phone: 860-928-2225
Products: peaches, local honey, and maple syrup

Meadowland Honey Bee Farm
Vibert Road, South Windsor, CT 06074
Phone: 860-869-6092 Email: meadowlandhoney@aol.com
Products: local wildflower honey from each of the three floral seasons, light spring honey, medium summer honey, and dark fall honey

Three Sisters Farms—Glenn Penkofflidbeck
11 Evans Lane, Essex, CT 06426
Phone: 860-767-7957 Email: info@threesistersfarm.com
Products: naturally grown wildflower and infused lavender honeys.

Tikkanen Berry Farm
218 Calvin French Road, Sterling, CT 06377
Phone: 860-77-0177
Products: red and black currants

Norman's Surgarhouse (Richard and Avis Norman)
387 County Road, Woodstock, CT 06281-2112
Phone: 860-974-1235 Email: r.norman@snet.net
Products: maple syrup year round, maple cream, native honey

Maple Lane Farms LLC
57 N.W. Corner Road, Preston, CT 06365
Phone: 860-887-8855 Email: allyn@maplelane.com
Products: red and black currants

Hurst Farm Sugar House
746 East Street, Andover, CT 06232
Phone: 860-646-6536
Products: maple syrup and maple products, local honey, herbs and spices

Lamothe's Sugar House
89 Stone Road, Burlington, CT 06013
Phone: 860-675-5043 Email: lomathes.sugar.house@sent.net
Mail order available at www.lamotesugarhouse.com
Products: maple syrup and maple products

Great Brook Sugarhouse (Mark Mankin)
140 Park Lane, Route 202, New Milford, CT 06776
Mailing Address: 50 East Street, New Milford, CT 06776
Phone: 860-354-0047
Products: maple syrup

Metric Conversion Chart

<u>Dimensions</u>

1/16 inch	= 2 mm
1/8 inch	= 3 mm
1/4 inch	= 6 mm
1/2 inch	= 1.5cm
3/4 inch	= 2 cm
1 inch	= 2.5 cm
4 inch	= 10 cm
8 inch	= 20 cm
9 inch	= 23 cm
10 inch	=25 cm

Oven <u>Temperatures</u>

200° F	95° C	very cool
225° F	110° C	very cool
250° F	120° C	very cool
275° F	135° C	cool
300° F	150° C	cool
325° F	160° C	warm
350° F	175° C	moderate
375° F	190° C	moderately hot
400° F	200° C	fairly hot
425° F	220° C	hot
450° F	230° C	very hot
475° F	245° C	very hot

<u>Weights</u>

1/4 ounce	= 7 grams
1/2 ounce	= 14 grams
3/4 ounce	= 21 grams
1 ounce	= 28 grams
2 ounce	= 57 grams
3 ounce	= 85 grams
4 ounce	= 113 grams
5 ounce	= 142 grams
6 ounce	= 170 grams
7 ounce	= 198 grams
8 ounce	= 227 grams
10 ounce	= 284 grams
12 ounce	= 340 grams
16 ounce	= (1 lb.) = 454 grams
35.25 ounce	= (2.2 lb.) =1 kilogram

Volume Measurements

Dry		Fluid	
1/8 tsp. =			0.5 ml
1/4 tsp. =			1 ml
1/2 tsp. =			2.5 ml
3/4 tsp. =			4 ml
1 tsp. =			5 ml
1 tbsp. =	3 tsp. =	0.5 fl. oz. =	15 ml
2 tbsp. =	6 tsp. =	1 fl. oz. =	30 ml
1/4 c. =	4 tbsp. =	2 fl. oz. =	60 ml
1/3 c. =	5 tbsp. + 1 tsp. =	2.5 fl. oz. =	75 ml
1/2 c. =	8 tbsp. =	4 fl. oz. =	125 ml
2/3 c. =	10 tbsp. + 2 tsp. =	5 fl. oz. =	150 ml
3/4 c. =	12 tbsp. =	6 fl. oz. =	175 ml
1 c. =	16 tbsp. =	8 fl. oz. =	250 ml
1 1/2 c. =	24 tbsp. =	12 fl. oz. =	375 ml
2 c. =	1 pint =	16 fl. oz. =	500 ml
3 c. =		24 fl. oz. =	750 ml
4 c. =	1 quart =	32 fl. oz. =	1 l
2 quarts =	1/2 gal. =	64 fl. oz. =	1.9 l
4 quarts =	1 gal. =	128 fl. oz. =	3.8 l
Pinch =	Less than 1/8 tsp.		

(Dry and Fluid)

Metric Conversion Formulas

To Convert	Multiply
Ounces to grams	Ounces by 28.35
Pounds to kilograms	Pounds by .454
Teaspoons to milliliters	Teaspoons by 4.93
Tablespoons ounces to milliliters	Tablespoons by 14.79
Fluid ounces to milliliters	Fluid ounces by 29.57
Cups to milliliters	Cups by 236.59
Cups to liters	Cups by .236
Pints to liters	Pints by .473
Quarts to liters	Quarts by .946
Gallons to liters	Gallons by 3.785
Inches to centimeters	Inches by 2.54

To convert Fahrenheit to Celsius, deduct 32 from Fahrenheit, then multiply result by 5, then divide by 9.

To convert Celsius to Fahrenheit, multiply Celsius by 9, then divide products by 5, then add 32.

Glossary

bain-marie. A bowl placed over a saucepan of simmering water; can substitute for a double boiler.

blending. A mixing method in which two or more ingredients are combined just until they are evenly distributed.

boil. To heat to the boiling point; to be in boiling water, which for water at sea level is 212°F (100°C).

brandy. An alcoholic beverage made by distilling the fermented mash of grapes or other fruits.

brown. To cook the surface until it is brown in color.

brown sugar. Regular, granulated sucrose (sugar) containing various impurities that give it a distinctive flavor.

buttercream. A light, smooth, fluffy frosting of sugar, fat, and flavoring; egg yolks or whipped egg whites are sometimes added. There are three principle kinds: simple, Italian, and French.

caramelize. The browning of sugars caused by heat; the browning of sugars enhances the flavor and appearance of foods.

compote. Cooked fruit served in its cooking liquid, usually a sugar syrup.

cream. The process of beating fat and sugar together to blend them uniformly and to incorporate air.

crème fraîche. A slightly aged, cultured heavy cream with a slightly tangy flavor that is very useful in cooking because it will not separate when boiled.

custard. A liquid that is thickened or set by the coagulation of egg protein.

dark chocolate. Sweetened chocolate that consists of chocolate liquor and sugar.

deglaze. To swirl or stir a liquid (usually wine or stock) in a sauté pan or other pan to dissolve cooked food particles remaining on the bottom; the resulting mixture often becomes the base for a sauce.

double boiler. A saucepan with a detachable upper compartment heated by simmering water in the lower one, used to protect foods from direct heat.

extracts. Concentrated mixtures of ethyl alcohol and flavoring oils such as vanilla, almond, and lemon.

flambé. Food served flaming: produced by igniting an alcoholic beverage to burn off alcohol and add flavor.

flour. A powdery substance of varying degrees of fineness made by milling grains such as wheat, corn, or rye.

fold. Incorporating light, airy ingredients into heavier ingredients by gently moving them from the bottom of the bowl to the top in a circular motion, usually with a rubber spatula.

formula. A recipe; the term is most often used in the bakeshop.

fruit. The edible organ that develops from the ovary of a flowering plant and contains one or more seeds.

garnish. An edible item added to another food as a decoration or accompaniment.

granulated sugar. Sucrose in a fine crystalline from.

grind. To pulverize or reduce food to small particles using a mechanical grinder or food processor.

hard sauce. A flavored mixture of confectioners' sugar and butter; often served with steamed puddings.

Kirsch. A clear alcoholic beverage distilled from cherries.

kosher. Describes food prepared in accordance with Jewish dietary laws.

liqueur. A strong, sweet, syrupy alcoholic beverage made by mixing or redistilling neutral spirits with fruits, flowers, herbs, spices, or other flavorings; also known as a cordial.

liquor. An alcoholic beverage made by distilling grains, vegetables, or other foods; includes rum, whiskey, and vodka.

macerate. Too soak foods in a liquid, usually alcoholic, for a period of time to soften them.

mise en place. French for "putting in place"; refers to the preparations and assembly of all necessary ingredients and equipment.

mix. To combine ingredients in such a way that they evenly disperse throughout the mixture.

molasses. The heavy brown sugar syrup made from sugar cane.

nut. The edible single-seed kernel of a fruit surrounded by a hard shell; generally, any seed or fruit with an edible kernel in a hard shell.

parchment paper. Heat resistant paper used throughout the kitchen for tasks such as lining baking pans, wrapping foods to be cooked en papillote and covering foods during shallow poaching.

purée. To grind, press, or strain to the consistency of a soft paste or thick liquid.

recipe. A set of written instructions for producing a specific food or beverage; also known as a formula.

reduce. To boil down and concentrate flavors and thicken liquids.

relish. A cooked or pickled sauce usually made with vegetables or fruits and often used as a condiment.

ripe. Fully grown and developed fruit; the fruit's flavor, texture, and appearance are at their peak and the fruit is ready to eat.

sauce. Generally, a thickened liquid used to flavor and enhance other foods.

simmer. To cook food gently in water or other liquid that is heated to the point at which bubbles are just breaking on the surface, maintaining the temperature of the liquid just below the boiling point.

spice. Any of a group of strongly flavored or aromatic portions of plants (or other leaves) used as flavoring, condiments, or aromatics.

springform pan. A circular baking pan with a separate bottom and a side wall held together with a clamp that is released to free the baked product.

stirring. A mixing method in which ingredients are gently mixed by hand until blended, usually with a spoon, whisk, or rubber spatula.

sucrose. The chemical name for regular granulated sugar and confectioners' sugar.

sugar. A carbohydrate that provides the body with energy and gives a sweet taste to foods.

syrup. Sugar that is dissolved in liquid, usually water, and often flavored with spices or citrus zest.

thickening agent. Ingredients used to thicken sauces; includes starches (flour, cornstarch, and arrow root), gelatin, and liaisons.

toss. To mix ingredients together lightly and gently.

water bath. A method of baking in the oven with a gentle moist even heat in which the pan of the product to be baked is placed into a larger pan filled with water and baked slowly.

whip. A mixing method in which foods are vigorously beaten in order to incorporate air; a whisk or an electric mixer with its whip attachment is used.

whisk. To stir or beat rapidly, with a light sweeping, aerating motion. (A whisk is a handheld beater consisting of a bulbous cage of wires attached to a handle.)

whole butter. Butter that is not clarified, whipped, or reduced in fat content; it may be salted or unsalted.

wine. An alcoholic beverage made from the fermented juice of grapes; may be sparkling (effervescent) or still (non-effervescent) or fortified with additional alcohol.

zest. The thin, colored oily layer of peel in a citrus fruit, which can be removed in paper-thin strips with a swivel-bladed vegetable peeler (or in a tiny julienne using a tool called a zester) or grated off with a fine grater.

Index

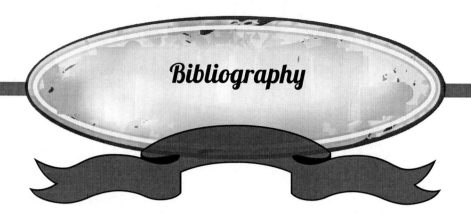

Bibliography

De Laurentiis, Giada. Food Network. 2011. www.foodnetwork.com/giada-de-laurentiis/index.html.

The Essential Dessert Cookbook. Vancouver, Bc, Canada: Whitecap Books, 2007

Evans, Dyfed Lloyd. *Traditional British Recipes*. Celtnet Recipes, 2005. celtnet.org.uk.

Fremlin, Maria. "How to Freeze Quinces." 2010. http://maria.fremlin.de/recipes/frozen-quinces.html.

Gisslen, Wayne. *Professional Baking, Third Edition*. New York: John Wiley & Sons, Inc., 2001.

Herbst Tyler, Sharon. The New Food Lover's Companion, Second Edition. Barron's Educational Series. 1995.

Stradley, Linda. What's Cooking America. 2004.

Tennant, Sarah. Tips for Perfect Baked Cheesecake. 2008.

White, Jasper. Cooking from New England. Newton, MA: Biscuit Books, Inc., 1998

Wilson, Carol. Traditional Scottish Recipes. London: Southwater, Anness Publishing Ltd, 2007, 2009.

Wolf, Burt. Burt Wolf's Menu Cookbook. Doubleday, 1998

Woodall, Diana Baker. Diana's Desserts. 2011.

Recipe Notes

Recipe Notes